TEA SHOP WALKS
IN
THE YORKSHIRE DALES

Clive Price

Published by Sigma Leisure – an imprint of
Sigma Press, 1 South Oak Lane, Wilmslow, Cheshire SK9 6AR, England.

British Library Cataloguing in Publication Data
A CIP record for this book is available from the British Library.

ISBN: 1-85058-599-7

Typesetting and Design by: Sigma Press, Wilmslow, Cheshire.

Cover photograph: Looking towards Redmire from Leyburn, Wensleydale *(Graham Beech)*

Maps: Redrawn by Alan Bradley, from sketches by the Author.

Photographs: the author

Printed by: MFP Design & Print

Disclaimer: the information in this book is given in good faith and is believed to be correct at the time of publication. No responsibility is accepted by either the author or publisher for errors or omissions, or for any loss or injury howsoever caused. Only you can judge your own fitness, competence and experience.

Acknowledgements

No book of this type is a solo effort. In this particular case I have been dependent on the help and assistance of several people.

My first debt of gratitude goes to Graham Beech and the staff of Sigma Leisure for their encouragement and suggestions and, using their expertise, for transforming my manuscript into the finished book.

Whenever school holidays permitted my granddaughter, Tamsin, has again proved to be an entertaining and observant companion, drawing my attention to the minutiae of the countryside which we adults often tend to overlook. My wife and daughters have encouraged and supported me and undertaken some of my domestic responsibilities whenever it has been necessary for me to be away from home for several days.

I must also thank the staff of the Yorkshire Dales National Park and the Tourist Information Centres in Ilkley, Skipton, Harrogate, Richmond, Ripon and Pateley Bridge for providing so much useful literature and for their patience in answering my innumerable queries.

A word of gratitude is due to all those farmers I have met along the way who have taken the time to have a conversation and, at the same time, to enlighten me on various aspects of their local countryside.

Finally, I am extremely grateful to all the tea shop owners and staff who have proved to be most friendly and co-operative while simultaneously providing some of the best fare it has been my privilege to taste. They have certainly lived up to Yorkshire's reputation for warm hospitality.

Clive Price

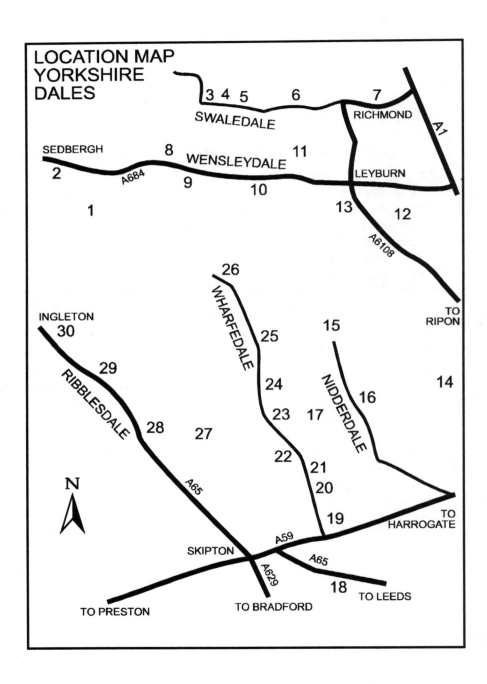

Contents

The Yorkshire Dales

The basic underlying geological feature of the Yorkshire Dales is lime-stone, formed millions of years ago when this area was part of a tropical sea, but with outcrops of sandstone, gritstone and shales. There are considerable areas of peat moorland, mainly around Ribblehead, Nid-derdale, Coverdale and Swaledale. All these variations provide a variety of scenery, especially for those who explore on foot.

These uplands are pierced by several rivers, their valleys normally carved out by the retreating glaciers of the Ice Age and since sculpted into their various shapes by the combined action of rain, frost, snow and wind. The Swale, the Ure, the Nidd, the Wharfe and the Aire flow southwards or eastwards to form the Yorkshire Ouse and Humber before entering the North Sea. The Dee and the Rawthey flow westwards to their confluence with the Lune while the Ribble, initially heads southwards before turning westwards into Lancashire and entering the Irish Sea.

These rivers and many smaller streams and becks flowing from the moorlands have created a series of waterfalls, or "Forces" as they are known locally, which attract increasing numbers of visitors every year. Water, too, has been responsible for the creation of all the caves, potholes and sink holes which pepper the Dales, a region which has developed into a mecca for the caver and the pot-holer. Human history has also done much to fashion this fabulous landscape. Evidence of Stone Age settlement has been unearthed at Yockenthwaite in Upper Wharfedale while the Romans exploited the lead deposits around Grassington and in Swaledale and Wensleydale. It was to safeguard these that they constructed a fort close to the present day village of Bainbridge in Wensleydale. Their road over Cam End into Ribblesdale and onwards to Ingleton and Lancaster is now popular with ramblers.

The Norse settlers bequeathed the Dales with a rich heritage of place-names ranging from Keld and Muker to Thwaite and Arkengarth-dale. They also introduced the name "Setter" into the English language through their practice of moving cattle and sheep onto higher pastures for summer grazing. This name is perpetuated in Countersett, Marsett, Burtersett and Apperset in Wensleydale. The tradition of the remote field barn, so much a feature of the landscape of the Dales, also derives from this ancient practice.

The Normans brought their castles to Middleham, Richmond and

Castle Bolton whilst simultaneously converting enormous tracts of land into hunting forests such as Langstrothsdale Chase and Middleham Moor, now used extensively for the training of racehorses.

During the Norman period the great and wealthy abbeys of Bolton, Jervaulx and Fountains were constructed. The monks acquired large estates throughout the Dales which they converted into ranges for their enormous flocks of sheep. In the more remote areas they established granges for the management of their holdings. To connect these with the mother house they developed a network of routes which still continue in use as green lanes. Mastiles Lane is one of the finest examples but there are many others. Similar green lanes are the result of the Scottish and North of England drovers guiding their flocks and herds southwards to the great cattle fairs.

Economic activity was not confined solely to agriculture: many of the Dales and surrounding hillsides are littered with the scars of lead mining. The flues, hushes, smelting houses and spoil heaps now blend into their surroundings to add a further point of interest to any walk. Some of these abandoned industrial sites have been specially preserved by the National Park. Coal, too, was mined on the moors surrounding Tan Hill, Ingleton and Upper Nidderdale. These industries, in their turn, created even more paths and tracks across a wide area. Some were turnpiked in the eighteenth century, as was the case with the road through Arkengarthdale from Reeth, but others survived simply as bridleways which still form a vital part of the footpath network.

Not surprisingly, in an area producing so much wool, the textile industry became fairly widespread with many of the villages boasting handloom weavers' cottages which still stand, admirable examples of vernacular architecture. The women of Dent, for example, acquired a reputation for the speed and quality of their hand-knitting.

As these traditional industries declined, the prosperity of many villages and small towns came to depend more and more on the development of tourism. Every summer thousands of people flock into the Dales to visit such renowned beauty spots as the Aysgarth Falls, Hardraw Force and Kilnsey Crag. Others are attracted by such historical remains as Richmond Castle, Middleham Castle, Fountains Abbey or Bolton Abbey.

Some come simply to escape from their urban environment whilst others love to wander through the streets, often cobbled, of some of the most picturesque villages to be found anywhere in England. Notable amongst these are Grassington and Dent. For large numbers of other people the Yorkshire Dales is a favoured walking area.

In 1953 the Yorkshire Dales National Park was established to conserve this unique landscape. It is responsible for maintaining all the footpaths within its boundaries and for protecting the landscape which it does through planning controls and creative management. Another duty is to help the visitor to enjoy quiet relaxation while, at the same time, allowing the farmers and other locals to get on with their work. This is often a fine balancing act which it carries out through its Ranger Service. The National Park has also built several Information Centres and car parks at popular spots to cater for the visitors. Over the centuries all these diverse elements have contributed in their own way to the creation of the landscape of the Yorkshire Dales which is different from the Lake District, the Peak District or from that of any other National Park. There is an indefinable quality which makes the Yorkshire Dales unique. It can be fully appreciated only by walking through the villages and out into the quieter, more tranquil valleys and onto the hills where nature may be experienced at first-hand.

The Walks

This collection of walks has been assembled to reveal not only the finest countryside to be found in England but also the rich variety from the high peat moorlands to the delightful riverside pastures. Scenic beauty has been the main consideration but some routes, or sections of routes, have been devised to permit visits to places of interest.

I have tried to vary the length and difficulty of each route so that there are many within the capability of almost everyone. This means that many are suitable for families with young children or for those who prefer something gentle. Even the most seasoned walker often enjoys an easier day. Where there are special difficulties involving navigation or severe climbing notice is given in the text.

Road walking has been kept to a minimum, although it is necessary occasionally to link footpaths to form a circular route. All the routes follow Public Rights of Way as shown on Ordnance Survey maps whether as paths or bridleways. In a few circumstances concessionary footpaths have been included following the recent introduction of various access schemes by the Countryside Commission, the privatised water companies, the Forestry Enterprise or Local Authorities. Stretches of footpath that are less frequently used may be difficult to detect on the ground. Where this is the case mention is made in the text and more minutely detailed navigational instructions included.

There is a great temptation in a book of this nature to include ascents of such popular summits as Ingleborough, Whernside and Pen-y-ghent but I have tried to avoid these in the interests of conservation. In recent years the National Park Authority has spent hundreds of thousands of pounds simply repairing the damage caused to these over-used paths. I have no desire to compound the problem by encouraging more boots to pound and so destroy an already fragile surface. I have used the same discretion in relationship to other popular and over-used routes. There are hundreds of miles of other paths simply waiting to be walked and they pass through equally attractive scenery.

Afternoon Tea

Afternoon Tea is quintessentially English. The very mention of the phrase conjures-up visions of wafer-thin cucumber sandwiches, stands of delectable scones, delicious cakes and cream accompanied by freshly-brewed tea served from an elegant silver pot. This idealised concept inspired several scenes in the plays of Oscar Wilde and prompted the poet, Rupert Brooke, to write:

"Stands the Church clock at ten to three?
And is there honey still for tea?"

Many hotels have transformed Afternoon Tea into a social ritual held against a background of light music provided by a pianist or even a small ensemble.

The English obsession with tea is a direct consequence of the conquest of India and Ceylon by Robert Clive and other British generals in the eighteenth century. Heavily promoted by the East India Company, it quickly ousted its chief rivals, coffee and chocolate, which were often regarded as the preferred beverages of our enemies of the period, the French and the Spanish. Tea drinking was equated with patriotism. In recent years its leading position has been challenged in this country by a revived interest in coffee but, so far, it has successfully resisted the threat.

Most English people will readily drink a cup of tea at any time of day on the flimsiest of excuses but late afternoon is still probably regarded as the favourite. To cater for this obsession, the country has developed a network of cafés, many of which are to be found in country villages. For reasons of viability they do not specialise in tea alone, but offer other beverages alongside cakes, scones, gateaux and light meals.

Everyone has their idea of what a country café should be but, as in other walks of life, times change and tea shops with them. The cosy establishment with linen tablecloths and bone china may still be found, but others are of the self-catering variety. All types will be found in this collection. Whatever the style of tea-room, the real criteria is that satisfying pot of tea accompanied by a cholesterol defying cream cake.

Some of the tea-rooms used in this book offer wide-ranging menus including full meals, while others provide snacks and similar refreshments depending on the time of day. For me, however, a pot of freshly-brewed tea, served with equally fresh scones, jam and cream, is the best way to round-off a day's walking in the countryside. And I know a lot of other walkers are of the same mind.

The opening times listed for each tea room were correct at the time of writing, and were re-checked as late as possible. However, circumstances change so, before embarking on your walk, it is advisable to check that nothing has altered. For this reason the telephone number, where applicable, has been included. Some cafés close completely during the winter months while others have restricted opening hours at week-ends only. In some cases tea rooms close permanently, either because of the expiry of a lease or because the owners wish to retire. Some may change owners with a subsequent change of style and menu.

Please Note: as an act of courtesy and common sense, please remove your muddy walking boots before entering. Many of the tea shops are luxuriously carpeted and do not exist solely to serve walkers. Again, for the convenience of other patrons, you may be requested to leave your rucksack outside. Most proprietors in the Yorkshire Dales welcome walkers and offer hospitality unequalled anywhere else in the country.

Tourist Information

The Yorkshire Dales are rich in tourist attractions ranging from the Ropemakers in Hawes to the glories of Bolton Castle and Fountains Abbey. Between these extremes come stately homes, small stone cottages with historical associations, pre-historic sites, Roman forts, 'Lost villages', ancient packhorse bridges, show caves, nature reserves and a multitude of craft workshops.

References to many of these are included in the text of the appropriate walk but there is no space in a book of this nature to provide detailed information. Small booklets and leaflets about most of these attractions are available at the local Tourist Information Centres which also sell souvenirs and Ordnance Survey maps.

For anyone wishing to stay for a few days these centres provide information about the various types of accommodation available in their particular areas ranging from four star hotels to farmhouse bed and breakfast and even camping barns. Tourist Information Centres also deal with queries relating to bus and train services, church services, shopping facilities and local events. The Yorkshire Dales National Park publishes a comprehensive "Accommodation Guide" which is updated annually. The principal Tourist Information Centres are to be found at:

Ilkley: Station Road. 01943 602319/436200.
Harrogate: Royal Baths Assembly Rooms,
                           Crescent Road 01423 525666.
Richmond: Victoria Road. 01748 850252.
Leyburn: Thornborough Hall, Leyburn. 01969 623069.
Skipton: 9, Sheep Street. 01756 792809.
Kirkby Lonsdale: Main Street. 015242 71437.
Settle: Town Hall, Cheapside. 01729 825192.

The Yorkshire Dales National Park has Visitor Centres which are open
daily between April and October, inclusive, from 10.00am to 5.00pm:

Aysgarth Falls: 01969 663424
Clapham: 015242 51419
Grassington: 01756 752774
Hawes: 01969 667450
Malham: 01729 830363
Reeth: 01748 884059
Sedbergh: 015396 20125

Clothing and Equipment

Even on the shortest walk good outdoor clothing will not only improve
your safety but also enhance your enjoyment. Obviously clothing is
often a matter of personal taste, but there are several general guidelines.

Jeans, for example, are not advisable in cold, wet weather because
they tend to increase the risk of hypothermia. Shorts are an acceptable
part of the outdoor scene in hot weather but increase the risk of sunburn
if the legs are exposed to bright sunshine for too long a period.

Most outdoor clothing shops offer a choice of walking trousers that
are suitable for most occasions but do remember that thicker ones, or
those lined with fleece, are advisable in winter and during colder
weather. Modern technology has produced clothing that is both light
and warm.

A good pair of walking boots or shoes is essential, even on lower
ground where paths can be exceptionally muddy, especially after rain,
or rocky and uneven. It is as easy to twist an ankle on lower ground as
it is on the summits. Boots have the advantage of providing extra
support for the ankles, especially when crossing stony or uneven
terrain. Any good stockist will offer a wide range at varying prices to
suit most pockets and the type of walking you intend to do. All will
offer advice. Avoid light shoes, high heels or sandals. Remember that
walking boots and shoes have a specially designed tread to improve
your grip in slippery conditions such as wet or frozen surfaces. It is also

suggested that you wear two pairs of socks, so allow for this when buying your boots. Most shops will loan a couple of pairs during fitting sessions.

Because the British climate is so fickle wet weather gear is essential. In recent years considerable improvements have been made in the types of material available including 'Gore-Tex' and other 'breathable' fabrics which tend to eliminate or reduce condensation. Again, a reputable stockist will proffer advice on what is available.

The variation in temperatures between the valley bottom and fell top indicates that it is advisable to carry an extra pullover in your rucksack. Clothing should not be too tight fitting or restrictive but reasonably loose and comfortable. The modern trend is to use 'Fleece" garments rather than woollen jumpers and there is now a range of lightweight but warm underwear on the market.

In colder weather the extremities such as fingers and ears should be covered because it is from these that most loss of body heat occurs. A warm, woolly hat which has flaps or can be pulled down over the ears is a must. So, too, are gloves.

Even on the shortest and lowest level walk always carry a first-aid kit. You are always at risk of minor cuts from barbed wire, bramble bushes and stone walls. Another invaluable item is a pocket knife. On most of these walks you are unlikely to encounter any major problems but, to call for assistance, a whistle is a useful aid.

Food also is a matter of personal taste but do ensure that at all times you carry some emergency rations in the form of chocolate or nutty bars which will provide sustenance and extra energy in case of delay.

To carry this essential equipment a day sack of 25 or 35 litres should prove more than adequate. To ensure that your spare clothing, food and others items remain dry in wet weather, it is a good idea to line the inside of the rucksack with a plastic bag.

Transport

Many people will travel to the start of each of these walks by car. For their benefit route directions have been supplied in the **Fact Section** at the beginning of each walk along with details of parking facilities.

To encourage greater use of public transport and so help to reduce traffic congestion in the National Park, details of bus and train services have been provided where applicable. These were correct at the time of writing but, since de-regulation, changes have been more frequent. Therefore it is advisable to check before starting out from home.

Many of the Dales are served by regular scheduled services. Other villages depend on buses which run only occasionally or even on specified days of the week. Some services, especially on Saturdays, Sundays and Bank Holidays, are subsidised by the National Park. These are usually known as "Dalesbuses" and normally start from towns and cities outside the National Park boundaries.

Skipton is served by frequent daily trains from Lancaster, Bradford, Leeds and Carlisle. Ilkley has a frequent service from Leeds and Bradford. The prolonged struggle to keep the Settle-Carlisle line open has finally been won, thereby maintaining a service which not only caters for the local inhabitants but also for the walker. On specified summer Sundays there are also through trains from Blackpool and Preston in addition to the regular trains between Leeds and Carlisle. Also, on specified days, there are bus services from certain stations on the Settle-Carlisle line to local villages in the Dales.

Intending visitors should obtain a copy of "Dales Connections". This guide is published by Elmtree Publications with support from the Yorkshire Dales National Park and details all services, both rail and bus. It is available from all National Park Centres or direct from the National Park Offices in Hebden Road, Grassington. A list of operators with their telephone numbers is given below.

British Rail

Lancaster:	01524 32333
Leeds:	0113 244 8133
Carlisle:	01228 44711
York:	01904 642155

Bus Operators

ABC Travel:	01704 576033
Bibby's Bus Co:	015242 41330
Burnley and Pendle Transport:	01282 425245
Cumberland Motor Services:	01946 63222
R. Harrington:	01969 650682
Harrogate and District Travel:	01423 56606
Hyndburn Transport:	01254 390816
Keighley and District Travel:	01535 603284
Kirkby Lonsdale Mini Coaches:	015242 72239
Pennine Motors:	01756 749215
Pride of The Dales:	01756 753123
Ribble Motor Services:	01524 424555
United Automobile Services:	01325 468771
J. Woof, Sedbergh:	015396 20414

Yorkshire Rider: 0113 2429614

Maps

The sketch maps included in the text are of a general nature. The route instructions should be followed in association with the appropriate Ordnance Survey map referred to in the **Fact Section**. The principal ones used in this book are as follows:

"The Yorkshire Dales: Western Area", number 2 in the O.S. "Outdoor Leisure" series.

"The Yorkshire Dales: Southern Area" : number 10 in the O.S. "Outdoor Leisure" series.

"The Yorkshire Dales: Northern and Central Areas", number 30 in the O.S. "Outdoor Leisure" series.

"Howgill Fells and Upper Eden Valley", number 19 in the O.S. "Outdoor Leisure" series.

"The Forest of Bowland and Ribblesdale" number 41 in the O.S. "Outdoor Leisure" series.

"Nidderdale". Number 26 in the O.S. "Explorer" series.

"Lower Wharfedale and Washburn Valley". Number 27 in the O.S. "Explorer" series.

"Middleham and Jervaulx Abbey", number 630 in the O.S. "Pathfinder" series.

"Richmond and Leyburn", number 609 in the O.S. "Pathfinder" series.

The two maps in the "Explorer" series, "Nidderdale" and "Lower Wharfedale and the Washburn Valley" have been published while this book has been in preparation. They are the same scale as the "Outdoor Leisure" maps but carry more tourist information and are especially good in showing recently negotiated Permissive Footpaths. In parts they duplicate the same areas as the "Outdoor Leisure" series.

May I wish everyone some excellent days out walking through this magical region followed by some delectable and mouth-watering refreshments in one of the many tea rooms to be discovered in the Yorkshire Dales.

Walk 1: Dent

A route through the gentler aspects of this delightful northern dale which also allows time to explore the quaint and ancient streets of Dent village.

Route: Dent – Church Bridge – Low Hall – Hall Bank – Scotchergill – Cross House – Tommy Bridge – Dent.

Start: National Park Car Park, Dent. Map reference 705871.

Distance: 5 miles (8km)

Map: "The Yorkshire Dales: Western Area", number 2 in the O.S. "Outdoor Leisure" series.

Public Transport: Dent Station, which is about 5 miles from the village, is served by daily (including Sunday) trains on the Leeds-Settle-Carlisle line. On Sundays bus service 566, operated by J. Woof, provides a direct link. For details phone 01288 812812.
There is a daily postbus service from Kendal and Sedbergh to Dent. (Not Sundays).

By Car: Dent is reached by a minor road signed from Sedbergh. Other unclassified roads provide links with Ingleton, Hawes and Kirkby Lonsdale. There is a National Park Car Park, (Pay and Display) in the village.

The Tea Shop

The Cobbled Close Tea Shop in Dent is housed in two seventeenth-century listed cottages close by the car park. This historical ambience is enhanced by the exposed wooden beams, low ceilings, flagged floors and two cast-iron ranges. Antique dressers and cupboards housing displays of old teapots and jars add to the olde-world atmosphere. Owned by Graham Hudson and Pat Barber, the Cobbled Close provides that informal atmosphere so essential to relaxing after a good walk.

Special dishes include Fisherman's Pie, Turkey Bean Pot, Liver and Bacon Pate, Oven-Baked Potatoes, Dalesman's Platter, Ham Salad and Homity Pie – a filling dish of cheese, onion and potato baked in a wholemeal pastry case.

The vast range of cakes, all made entirely on the premises, includes Buttered Scone, Chocolate Cake, Coffee Cake, Farmhouse Fruit Cake, Date and Walnut Cake, Carrot Cake and Yorkshire Curd Tart. For that special treat there is French Bread Pudding with whisky sauce and cream. The list of speciality teas ranges from Yorkshire to Gunpowder and includes Jasmine and Lapsang Souchong. The most unusual beverage is Happy Marriage – a mixture of Hot Chocolate and Coffee topped with Whipped Cream. Opening hours: Mid-March to November: Daily: 10.30am to 5.30 pm. December to mid March: Saturdays and Sundays only: 10.30am to 5.30 pm. Phone : 015396 25231.

Dent

With its narrow, twisting cobbled streets and old stone cottages huddled closely together around St Andrew's church, Dent is arguably the most attractive village in the Yorkshire Dales National Park. Until 1974 it was located within the former West Riding but, for some reason beyond the understanding of ordinary mortal men, the bureaucrats decided to transfer it into the new county of Cumbria. The Yorkshire traditions live on, however. Mileposts and signposts, for instance, still retain the logos of the former Local Authority, perhaps as a form of regional defiance. Fortunately, Dent remains within the Yorkshire Dales National Park.

It is the only significant settlement in the

Dent

Dee Valley, testimony to the Norse origins of this area because the Vikings preferred living in isolated settlements such as some of those passed on the route of this walk. Today Dent is a quiet tourist mecca of some 600 inhabitants but this was not always the case. In 1800, when it had a population of 1,773, it boasted a thriving textile industry producing gloves and stockings made by "The Terrible Knitters of Dent". This strange title did not imply an inferior quality of work but rather to the speed at which the women plied their needles. Allegedly they were so rapid that sparks flew. Some of the wooden galleries attached to the first floors of the houses where the knitters sat may still be seen.

Dent is also famous as the birthplace of Adam Sedgwick, recognised as the father of modern geology. The son of the Rector, he attended Dent Grammar School, which still stands in the churchyard, and the nearby Public School at Sedbergh before proceeding to Cambridge University where, eventually, he rose to be a professor. A fountain commemorating him, set in Shap granite, occupies a prominent position in the centre of the village.

Dent Marble is a special limestone which, when polished, becomes very attractive. During the nineteenth century it was in great demand for fireplace surrounds, table-tops and ornaments. The floor between the choir stalls and sanctuary of St Andrew's church is paved with this local product.

Standing at 1,150 feet above sea level, Dent station on the Settle-Carlisle line, is the highest in England.

The Route

Turn left out of the car park entrance to pass the Cobbled Court Tea Room on your left on your way into the village centre. By Sedgwick's Memorial and "The George and Dragon" fork left, soon leaving the houses behind. At the far end of Church Bridge make a left turn through a gated stile, descend a short flight of steps and follow the riverside path to the far end of the field. Nearing the corner, where the River Dee curves away to the left, bear right to a footpath sign and stile to join a narrow, surfaced lane.

Go left for 200 metres and then turn right into the entrance to Low Hall and High Hall. After 10 metres, and by a footpath sign, turn right through a gated stile and cross the lower part of the field to a wooden five-barred gate. The slopes of North Lord's Land are to the left and Crag Hill to the right.

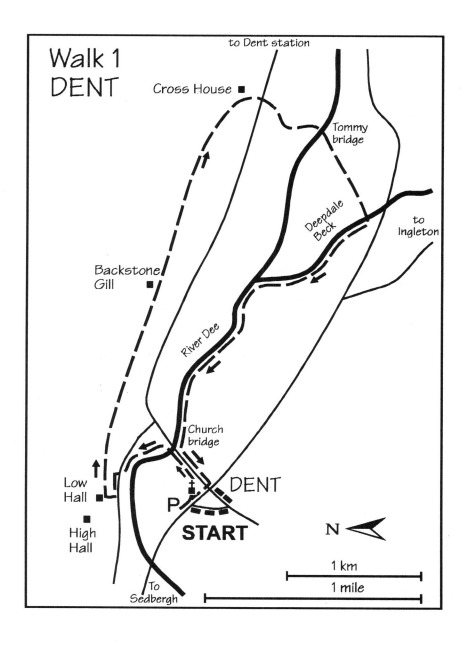

Maintain the same line of direction through a metal five-barred gate to pass to the right of a partially white house to reach a waymarked five-barred gate. Cross the driveway diagonally for 5 metres to a way-marked gated stile and traverse the next field with a substantial stone house, "Dee View", away to the your left.

Cross another driveway to a metal five-barred gate and then veer towards the right-hand corner of the ensuing field to find a squeezer stile in the corner. Bear left towards another waymarked five-barred gate before staying to the left of a farm to another five-barred gate. Continue forwards, crossing a bridge spanning a stream to yet another five-barred gate after 10 metres and then aim for a white cottage with another gate alongside at Hall Bank.

Pass between the white cottage on your right and a row of cottages, the former Dent Workhouse, to a waymarked gate. Advance 5 metres and, immediately in front of a barn, turn left for 5 metres and then turn right to a through stile located to the left of a five-barred gate. Proceed to the left of the stone wall and, where this terminates, maintain the same line of direction alongside a fence and some trees to an incon-spicuous small wooden gate. Through this turn left along a track and, after 10 metres, bend towards the right to pass a large stone barn and another small white cottage, both on your left.

From this point onwards there are some excellent views of Aye Gill Pike, above to the left, and Great Knoutberry Hill directly ahead. In the far distance Whernside is easily distinguished. It is rewarding to enjoy these views without all the effort of climbing.

Continue to the right of a wall and, where this ends, continue ahead to a metal five-barred gate and then turn right along another track before cornering a stone cottage to reach a T-junction in front of a converted barn. Turn left. After 7 metres go to the right, cross a wooden footbridge and, at the far end, turn right and then immediately left into a walled lane which leads to a waymarked white metal gate.

Just before reaching a cream-coloured house, "East Bakestonegill", turn right to a waymarked T-junction. Turn left, pass in front of the house to a waymarked gate. Beyond this, on reaching a boundary wall, turn left up a slope which has a handrail for a distance of about six metres to reach a wicket gate. Through this turn right. Proceed to the left of a wall to another gated stile and, after a further 100 metres go right through another gated stile and then left for a further 12 metres to a waymarked fence.

Stay to the left of this and to the right of a spasmodic row of hawthorns to a squeezer stile. Cross the stone clapper bridge before heading across the grass for about 20 metres to a through stile in Scotcher Gill, land once owned by the monks of Coverham Abbey near Middleham.

Continue along the higher part of the next field to a gated stile and then aim for a large tree which sports a traditional wooden stile right by its base. Proceed to a conspicuous ladder stile to the right of some farm outbuildings and stay forward to the left of a fence-cum-hedge before passing behind a house to a waymarked wall corner.

Remain with the boundary wall as it curves round to the right to reach a squeezer stile in the facing wall. Retain the same bearing across the next field, passing a derelict barn growing trees, to gain a waymarked stone step stile. Proceed forwards through a decrepit hedged field boundary and stay to the right of a house to meet another track.

Turn right, negotiate a waymarked gateway, cross a cattle grid and walk behind "Cross House" before following the driveway until meeting the Dent to Cowgill and Hawes road.

Turn right along this but, after 15 metres, fork right along a signed bridleway. Go through a large metal five-barred gate and stay to the right of the farm buildings before negotiating a second. Bear right whilst staying to the right of a fence-cum-hedge as you descend a waymarked slope to a wooden five-barred gate. Remain to the right of the subsequent wall and, where it terminates, maintain the same line to reach Tommy Bridge, a wooden affair spanning the River Dee.

On the far side turn right to pass through a metal five-barred gate. On approaching a second, negotiate a stile some 10 metres to the left, and climb a steep slope with a wall on your left to meet a footpath finger post. Taking your direction from the arm of this post, use the series of waymarker posts to guide you across the large field before descending to a ladder stile alongside Bridge End Farm, which permits access to the road from Dent to Ingleton.

Turn right over the bridge and Deepdale Beck. After 100 metres turn right along the path signed to Church Bridge and which forms a stretch of the Dales Way, a long distance route from Ilkley to Windermere.

Ahead are the rounded summits of the Howgill Fells. The path, alongside Deepdale Beck and, later, the River Dee is clear and distinct as it negotiates a series of stiles and gates to reach Church Bridge on the outskirts of Dent. Turn left along the road for the Cobbled Corner and, after refreshments, the car park.

Walk 2: Sedbergh

With the rounded summits of the Howgill Fells as a constant
backdrop this route explores the Rawthey valley.

Route: Sedbergh – Castlehaw – Underbank – Stone Hall – Ellerthwaite –
                         Buckbank – Straight Bridge – New Bridge – Sedbergh.

Start: Joss Lane Car Park, Sedbergh. Map reference 659922.

Distance: 4 miles (6.5km).

Maps: 1. "Howgill Fells and Upper Eden Valley", number 19 in the O.S.
                         "Outdoor Leisure" series. 2. "Yorkshire Dales: Western Area", num-
                         ber 2 in the O.S. "Outdoor Leisure" series.

Public Transport: Bus service 564, Brough – Kirkby Stephen – Sedbergh – Kendal.
                         Mondays to Saturdays.
                         Frequent between Sedbergh and Kendal. Cumberland Bus Com-
                         pany and J. Woof.
                         Bus service 566, Sedbergh to Dent Station. Sundays only. J. Woof.
                         Dalesbus service 804/805. Leeds – Bradford – Skipton – Hawes –
                         Sedbergh. Summer Sundays and Bank Holidays only. Keighley and
                         District Bus Company.

By Car: Sedbergh is located on the A684 Northallerton to Kendal road, some
                         5 miles east of Junction 37 on the M6 motorway. There are several
                         car parks in the town centre.

The Tea Shop

The Posthorn Tea and Coffee Shop, which is situated in Sedbergh's
Main Street, is steeped in history. The premises were formerly "The
King's Arms", a celebrated coaching hostelry where, twice daily, the
horses were changed on the Lancaster to Newcastle coach. The Dick-
ensian atmosphere has been preserved with the thick oak beams, stone
fireplace and cast-iron urn. The thick, stone walls are decorated with a
floral paper which blends with the displays of Willow-Patterned crock-
ery. The dark wooden shelves behind the counter house an array of
old-fashioned tins and jars containing numerous varieties of teas and
coffees. Step into the Posthorn and you step back almost 200 years into
history. It stands opposite the Library, formerly the Literary Institute,

and the Parish Church of St Andrew while commanding delightful views of the Frostrow and Middleton fells.

The Posthorn offers one of the widest ranges of coffee served by any tea shop in the Dales offering French, Columbian, Sumatra, Mandheling, Cuban, Yemen 'Ismaili', Italian Roast, Brazilian Santos and Costa Rican. This is matched by an equally impressive list of speciality teas.

For any walker in search of real sustenance there is "The Coachman's Grill" which is specially designed "For the Hungry Traveller". It includes Rump Steak, Cumberland Sausage, Gammon, Black Pudding, Eggs, Pineapple, Tomato, Chips and Peas. If eating that appears to be something of a Herculean task there is a choice from Plaice, Haddock, Cumberland Sausage, Cheese or Beans on Toast. Another alternative is "The Dales All-Day Breakfast", another gargantuan repast designed for true trenchermen.

Even Afternoon Tea offers a challenge with sandwiches, scones with jam and cream and two cakes of choice from the display. Everything is freshly prepared and cooked on the premises by Alan and Chris Clowes whose mouth-watering cakes include, amongst many others, Fruit Pies, Sticky Toffee Pudding, Jam Roly Poly, Lemon Cheesecake, Chocolate Cake, Carrot Cake, Flapjack and Shortcake. Opening times: Daily, all year: 9.00am to 5.30pm. Phone 015396 21389.

The Posthorn Tea Shop

Sedbergh

With a population of 2,500 Sedbergh is the largest town in the Yorkshire Dales National Park although, ironically, since 1974 it has been in Cumbria. The name is derived from the Norse, "Setberg", which translates as "Flat Topped Hill", an obvious reference to Winder and the other rounded fells which comprise the Howgills and which protect the town on its northern side. The Normans erected a motte-and-bailey castle on Castlehaw in the north-western corner of the town but little of this defensive work remains today. The Parish Church of St Andrew is also of Norman origin while the market, still held every Wednesday on Joss Street car park, has been functioning continuously since the grant of a charter in 1251.

Apart from trade in livestock, the town's wealth was based on the textile industry, especially hand-knitting. The narrow alleyways, crammed between Main Street and Back Street, once boasted wooden galleries where, as in nearby Dent, the knitters sat while plying their trade.

Above all, Sedbergh is perhaps most famous for its Public School whose playing fields cover several acres on the south side of the town. Established in 1525 by Roger Lupton, a native of Sedbergh and Provost of Eton, it was rebuilt in 1716 and became a Public School in 1874. Of its more recent pupils perhaps the most famous is Will Carling, the English rugby captain.

The National Park Information Centre on Main Street, has town plans, maps and booklets. Phone: 015396 20125.

The Route

Leave Joss Lane car park by the National Park Information Centre and turn left along Main Street for approximately 100 metres. By the inverted Y road junction with Back Lane make a left turn into the unsigned Castlehaw Lane, soon passing "Town End Cottage". Beyond the few houses the walled lane climbs gently through trees before emerging into more open countryside and reaching Castlehaw Farm. On the far side of the first wooden five-barred gate turn right, as suggested by the waymarker on the barn, and proceed in front of the house to a three-armed footpath post, crossing a small bridge on the way.

By this sign turn right in the direction of "Gyll Farm" and pass through a metal five-barred gate with the slopes of Winder rising

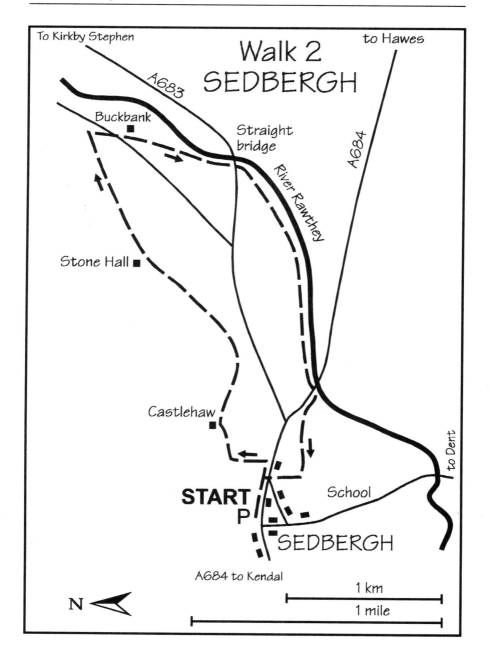

sharply on your immediate left. Pass to the right of an old barn to a squeezer stile and through that turn right down a slight slope to a more traditional wooden stile which permits entry into a woodland.

Walk the clear path through the trees, descend a short flight of steps and cross a stream to another stile. Continue now to the left of the trees with a stream flowing through the wooden clough on your right.

At the T-junction with a wider track go right before quickly losing altitude to a metal kissing gate by another three-armed footpath sign. Turn left along the bridleway to "Underbank", enjoying a splendid prospect along Dentdale to Whernside.

Beyond a metal five-barred gate pass between the buildings at "Underbank", the white farmhouse being on your left, to reach another T-junction.

Turn right through a waymarked five-barred gate to follow the broad track for approximately 100 metres. Where this bends round to the right, leave the track leftwards to a wooden stile by a five-barred gate. Continue forwards over the next field, aiming for the apparent curve of a distant stone wall on your left. Where the wall terminates, stay to the right of the fence to a stile and footbridge.

Proceed in the same direction but now to the left of a wall and, in the far corner of the field, make a right turn through a somewhat inconspicuous stile by a broken gate to emerge onto the driveway leading to Stone Hall with its strange chimneys.

Turn left along the driveway but, at the Y-junction after 25 metres, bear right, as directed by a waymark, and cross a cattle grid to come face-to-face with a rather large barn sporting an interesting weather vane in the form of a bird with a feather.

There, turn right through a wooden five-barred gate and then immediately left, again as advised by a waymark. Pass to the right of the gable-end of the barn and, afterwards, of a wall.

Negotiate a stile in the right-hand field corner and turn right over a footbridge before veering leftwards towards "Hollin Hill House" which carries the date, 1712.

In front of the house bear left, as per the waymark, to a step stile behind the barn before heading towards a ladder stile in the right-hand corner of the field. Over that stay to the right of a hedge to a traditional wooden stile and continue along the same bearing to pass to the left of a 20-metre length of stone wall protruding from the fence on your right. Next, aim for a wooden stile on the right and, having passed behind a white house, turn right to reach a footpath sign with a stile alongside. This provides access to a surfaced lane.

Turn right for a short distance but, by "Buckbank Farm" and a partially hidden footpath sign to "Straight Bridge ⅜ mile", bear left through a large, white metal gate. Stay to the right of the farmhouse and then corner the barn on your right. At the far end of the barn turn left and pass the cattle pens to a metal five-barred gate.

Advance some 20 metres to one of the wooden variety and continue alongside a fence on your left to a somewhat obscure wooden stile hidden by a small dip in the ground but some 6 metres to the left of a conspicuous waymark. Proceed to the right of a fence and wall to a stone step stile and the A683, the road from Sedbergh to Kirkby Stephen, at the western end of Straight Bridge.

Exercising extreme caution, cross the road directly to another footpath sign and a through stile before descending a flight of stone steps onto the clear path which forms part of the Rawthey Way.

At the far end of the first field climb a very tall ladder stile which is followed immediately by another flight of steps to a wooden stile at the top. From this point there are no navigational problems. The path, using several stiles and footbridges, runs alongside the River Rawthey until reaching New Bridge on the A684, the Sedbergh-Hawes road.

Turn right along this for approximately 200 metres and the 30 mph signs. A few metres beyond these turn left into a lane. By "The Old Vicarage" stay forward through a squeezer stile and pass to the left of the house, A part of Sedbergh School is to your left.

By the T-junction turn right into Vicarage Lane which, eventually emerges onto Back Lane. Cross directly and, almost immediately, turn left into Main Street for a return to the car park. The Posthorn is but a short distance further.

Walk 3: Thwaite

A short but strenuous route in the remoter areas of Upper Swaledale. Because of parking problems it is advisable to start from Muker where there is a small pay and display car park.

Route: Muker – Kisdon – Doctor Wood – Dungeon – Thwaite – Usha Gap Bridge – Muker.

Start: Car Park, Muker, Swaledale. Map reference 911978.

Distance: 3½ miles (5.75km)

Map: "The Yorkshire Dales: Northern and Central Areas", number 30 in the O.S. "Outdoor Leisure" series.

Public Transport: Bus service number 30, Richmond – Gunnerside – Muker – Keld. Tuesdays and Saturdays only. United Bus Company.

By Car: Muker is located on the B6270 road between Richmond and Kirkby Stephen. From Hawes it may be approached by an unclassified road over the Buttertubs Pass. There is a small Pay and Display car park at the eastern entrance to the village.

The Tea Shop

Standing in the centre of the tiny upland settlement of Thwaite at the head of Swaledale, the Kearton Tea Rooms take their name from the two famous wildlife photographers who were born in Thwaite. With their bow windows and white walls, they offer a warm invitation to all who tramp the local hills and dales. Inside, the surprisingly large L-shaped room is pervaded by an air of luxury, the far section being a licensed restaurant. All the windows command stunning views of Swaledale and Kisdon Hill.

The menu is comprehensive and includes Soup of the Day, Jacket Potatoes, Sandwiches, Scampi, Plaice or Beef Pasty. The Cream Tea with scones, preserves and cream are a speciality of the house, as are the Blueberry Muffins and Danish Pastries. The extensive range of cakes is baked on the premises. Beverages include tea, coffee and hot chocolate in addition to soft drinks. Opening times: March to early January:

The Kearton Guest House and Tea Shop

daily, 10.00am to 5.00pm. Closed most of January and February. Phone 01748 886277.

Thwaite

The tiny settlement of Thwaite is nothing more than a cluster of stone-built houses sheltered by the bulk of Kisdon Hill in Upper Swaledale. It was the birthplace of the Kearton brothers, the noted wildlife photographers who learned the rudiments of their craft in the local fields and woods.

The Route

From the car park entrance turn left along the B6270, crossing the infant Swale by the old stone bridge and proceeding towards the centre of Muker village. Bear right by the Literary Institute and, in front of the adjacent Public Hall, veer left. By the Post Office go to the left again and, after 10 metres, turn right for a further 10 metres to a footpath finger post indicating a route to Keld.

Pass to the right of Lane Farm and then to the left of a house, "Breconside", before negotiating a wooden five-barred gate. The rough bridleway then twists and turns as it climbs steeply up the southern flank of Kisdon Hill to offer ever-expanding views down the length of Swaledale with Black Moor and Ivelet Moor to the right.

At the end of one straight stretch ignore a through stile on your left, remaining with the bridleway as it corkscrews upwards through another wooden five-barred gate beyond which the moorlands of Upper Swaledale come into view. On reaching a Pennine Way sign by an isolated farm, turn left. **Do not go right** because this leads to Keld.

After 50 metres meet another footpath sign adjacent to a five-barred gate. Again **ignore the sign to Keld** – do not go through the gate. Instead, turn left into a walled lane, signed "Pennine Way", to reach yet another five-barred gate and Pennine Way sign. Bear right for 5 metres to a second gate which has "To Thwaite" written on it in white paint.

Pass to the right of Kisdon House and, keeping a wall on your left, follow a green lane with an excellent grassy walking surface. Doctor's Wood is now on your left. At the next footpath sign, by the end of a wall and a few metres before a barn, veer leftwards as you descend heather-covered moorland on a narrow path and passing two stone cairns on your way to yet another Pennine Way sign by a stile. This area is shown on the map as "Dungeon".

Turn left through this stile to drop down the field to the immediate right of a wall. At the bottom swing right to keep a beck on your left for a distance of about 50 metres before turning left through a metal five-barred gate. Cross the beck by a small, stone-arched bridge.

Stay forward across the centre of the field to a rusty metal five-barred gate and then continue towards the farm and a footpath sign with a stile adjacent. Continue to the left of a wall before swinging left to a through stile by the corner of a house. Turn right for the Kearton Tea Rooms.

Suitably refreshed, retrace your steps to the Pennine Way sign at the third stile. At this point the long distance route heads off towards the left. However, your route stays forward along the line indicated by a "FP Muker" sign. With Kisdon Hill away to your left, follow the distinct path along the left bank of a beck to a through stile and then maintain direction to another, this time to the right of a field barn.

Stay forward to the end of the wall on your left and a squeezer stile. From there the path runs to the right of another beck to reach a small wooden gate. Through this turn left over a footbridge to a gated stile and then right to walk to the left of another wall to a gated stile. Beyond, bear right to an obvious gap between a barn on your left and a wall-end on your right. Through this veer left to another gated stile and stay forward to the right of a wall and then to the right of a barn to a footpath sign with a stile adjacent.

This permits an exit onto the B6270 at Usha Gap. Turn left along the road for a few metres and turn left into the entrance to Usha Gap Farm and another footpath sign. By this turn right through a stile and bear left while staying to the right of a barn to reach the diagonally opposite corner of the field and a gated stile some 7 metres to the right of a five-barred gate.

Turn right through this stile and proceed to the left of a wall to another gated stile in the field corner. Continue, still to the left of a wall which, at one point has a cattle trough ingeniously set into it so that cattle from the two fields may use it.

Maintain the same line of direction through a series of stiles until the path becomes flagged and emerges between the houses by the Post Office in the centre of Muker. From there retrace your steps to the car park unless you wish to enjoy a second cup of tea at the Muker Tea Rooms.

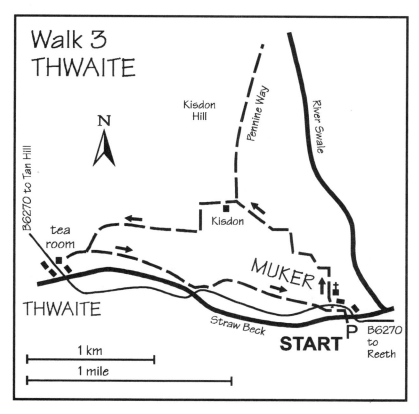

Walk 4: Muker

Still in Upper Swaledale, this high level traverse above the river leads to a historic bridge before a return through riverside pastures.

Route: Muker – Kisdon Scar – Calvert Houses – Ivelet Heads – Gunnerside Lodge – Ivelet Bridge – Ramps Holme – Muker.

Start: Car park, Muker, Swaledale. Map reference 911978.

Distance: 6 miles (9.5km)

Map: "The Yorkshire Dales: Northern and Central Areas", number 30 in the O.S. "Outdoor Leisure" series.

Public Transport: Bus service number 30, Richmond – Gunnerside – Muker – Keld. Tuesdays and Saturdays only. United Bus Company.

By Car: Muker is located on the B6270 road between Richmond and Kirkby Stephen. From Hawes it may be approached by the unclassified road over the Buttertubs Pass. There is a small Pay and Display car park at the eastern entrance to the village.

The Tea Shop

The Muker Tea Shop and Village Store, both run by David and Gwen May, are housed next to each other in the former vicarage. They may not dispense much spiritual succour these days, but they certainly appreciate how to cater for the inner needs of men and women who have been tramping the Swaledale fells all day. With its two cosy rooms seating 30 people, and the outdoor patio for those sunny days, accommodating a further 12, there is ample space for the largest party.

Using mainly local ingredients, everything from the Swaledale Curd Tart to the Beef and Kidney Pie is cooked by Gwen on the premises. The Curd Tart is a satisfying mixture of curds, cheese and currants soaked in rum. Their Yorkshire Rarebit is a local cheese soaked in Brown Ale, cooked and served on a thick slice of ham.

Theakston's Old Peculier Fruit Cake is, as you would expect, accompanied by a generous portion of Swaledale Cheese. For anyone searching for a rather less exotic dish there is Banana and Ginger Cake, Scones

The Tea Shop, Muker

served with amazingly large helpings of preserves and cream, Afternoon Tea and Cream Tea. In addition to their Thick Vegetable Soup there is a choice of Balti meals, Lasagne, Butterfly Chicken Breast, Salmon Steak, Welsh Rarebit, Filled Yorkshire Puddings, Omelettes, Salads and Sandwiches. Not surprisingly there is a daunting range of speciality teas and coffees. Opening times: Easter to the end of October 10.30am to 5.00pm. Closed Wednesdays and Thursdays. November to Easter: Saturdays and Sundays, 10.30am to dusk. Phone 01748 886409.

Muker

Muker, pronounced "Mooker", is a name derived from the Norse meaning "a cultivated enclosure", an accurate description for this fertile spot embraced by sweeping moorlands. One of the most attractive villages in Swaledale, it is dominated to the north-west by the bulk of Kisdon Hill. The tiny huddle of stone houses and cottages, centred around the sixteenth-century church, stands on the slopes above the Swale. Apart from the church, Muker boasts two other locally famous buildings – the tiny Public Hall and the Literary Institute, both of which are still in regular use providing a focal point for the social life of the village.

As with so many villages in Swaledale, Muker was closely associated with the lead mining industry until the nineteenth century but its pride and joy today is its Silver Band which celebrated its centenary in 1997 with a string of concerts and recordings.

The meadows along the river in both directions attract wild flower experts from all parts of the world, especially in late Spring and early Summer, while a stroll along one of the many riverside paths through this botanist's paradise is a sheer delight.

Commemorative plaques on the chapel in Muker recall Richard and Cherry Kearton, two of the world's first wildlife photographers who, though born in nearby Thwaite (see Walk 3), attended school in Muker.

Ivelet Bridge, featured in this walk, is an old packhorse bridge which formed part of the Corpse Road which ran from Keld and Thwaite to Grinton. In the days before Muker acquired its own church, bodies were carried from the remoter areas of Upper Swaledale to the church at Grinton for burial. The large, flat stone on the parapet was used as a resting stage for the biers or coffins.

The Route

From the car park entrance turn left along the B6270, crossing the River Swale by the ancient stone bridge and proceeding towards the centre of the village. By the minuscule Literary Institute bear right and, in front of the Lilliputian Public Hall, veer left. On gaining the Post Office after a few metres, go to the right for about 10 metres before turning left by a footpath finger post indicating routes to Gunnerside and Keld.

Negotiate the stile by a five-barred metal gate and stay forward over the field to a gated stile after which the clear path bears right. By the far corner of a field barn curve left to a squeezer stile before traversing several other narrow fields using a series of gated stiles until reaching the banks of the Swale.

Turn right, descend a short flight of steps and proceed to the right of the river for a few metres to Ramps Holme footbridge. Turn left over this and, reaching the far side of the river, turn right along the path signed to Gunnerside. Proceed a further 50 metres to a T-junction. Turn right. After another 100 metres, and just before a field barn, the path forks. Take the left-hand path which is signed "To Gunnerside By Road". Immediately embark on a diagonal climb to meet a wide track. Turn right along this, climbing steeply to pass just below Kisdon Scar, Low Kisdon and Cock Crow Scar, a series of limestone escarpments some of which, judging by the enormous blocks of stone cluttering the steep slopes, show sign of recent erosion, probably due to the weather.

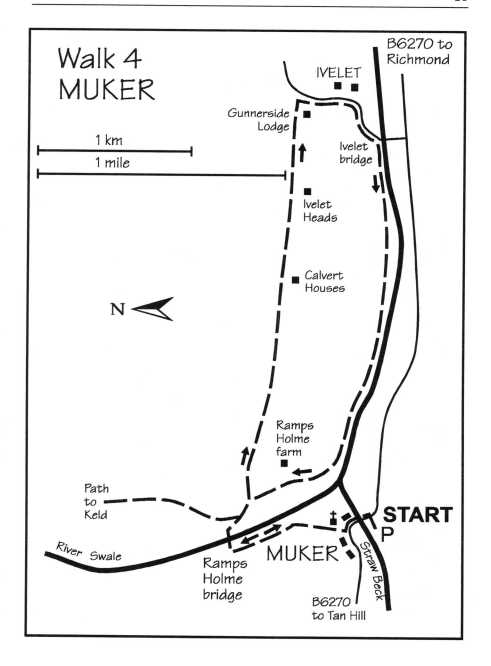

Walk 4
MUKER

1 km
1 mile

B6270 to
Richmond

IVELET

Gunnerside
Lodge

Ivelet
bridge

Ivelet
Heads

N

Calvert
Houses

Ramps
Holme
farm

Path
to
Keld

START
P

River Swale

Ramps
Holme
bridge

MUKER

Straw Beck

B6270
to Tan Hill

Far below to the right, there is a magnificent prospect down Swaledale, more than ample reward for the long climb.

A slight descent carries you by Calvert Houses before another ascent leads out onto heather moorland. After passing "Ivelet Heads", a squat stone cottage in a most exposed position, the track descends steeply to a T-junction by the impressive Gunnerside Lodge at the head of Shore Gill. Turn right to corkscrew down the hill on a narrow, surfaced road to a Y-junction by a telephone kiosk. Fork right. Ignore a path signed to Muker on your right. Instead, continue along the narrow road as it bends to the right to accompany the Swale. Where the road bends through 90 degrees to the left for the crossing of Ivelet Bridge, pass through a small facing gate at the northern end of the bridge with a footpath sign alongside. *Do not cross Ivelet Bridge.*

Beyond the first gateway, keep forward along the bottom of a ridge, past the end of a wall to a waymarked small gate some 100 metres to the right of the River Swale. Continue to the left of another waymarked wall-end as the path crosses a stretch of delightful greensward with a field barn a short distance to your right. Bear slightly to the right onto a riverside terrace to negotiate a gated stile, followed by a gap in a derelict wall by a barn, and then pass through a waymarked gate.

Through this walk to the left of a fence and just above the river. On meeting a footpath sign, veer right onto a diversion arising from the erosion of the original riverside path. After 150 metres, negotiate a wooden stile and advance a further 20 metres to a footpath sign as the wider path, now a grass track, follows the course of the river with piping oystercatchers on the shingle banks.

Beyond a waymarked gated stile stay forward for 100 metres to the right of the fencing to another footpath sign, this time adjacent to a stile in the fence. Over this turn left and then right, so that the fence is on your right and the river on your left. After a short distance the path acquires fences on both sides until reaching a waymarked gated stile.

From this swing diagonally right across the field to a green five-barred gate. Follow the clear path as it runs along a terrace to another gated stile, this time to the left of a cottage. Bear right towards a green metal five-barred gate, a barn and a gated stile all adjacent to each other.

Advance 50 metres to a footpath finger post to re-join your outward route. Retrace your steps to Ramps Holme footbridge and then across the fields into the centre of Muker.

Walk 5: Gunnerside

After exploring the dramatic gorge of the lower reaches of Gunnerside Gill, we climb onto Gunnerside Pastures before returning to the village.

Route: Gunnerside – Gunnerside Gill – Birbeck Wood – Middle Bank – Jingle Pot Edge – Gunnerside Pastures – Gunnerside.

Start: Parking area alongside Gunnerside Beck opposite the Post Office. Map reference, 943982.

Distance: 3½ miles (5.25km)

Map: "The Yorkshire Dales: Northern and Central Areas", number 30 in the O.S. "Outdoor Leisure" series.

Public Transport: Bus service number 30. Richmond – Gunnerside. Mondays to Saturdays. United Bus Company.

By Car : Gunnerside is located on the B6270 road between Richmond and Kirkby Stephen which runs through Swaledale. This road is linked to the A684 through Wensleydale by several minor roads. There is limited parking by Gunnerside Gill in the centre of the village.

The Tea Shop

The Ghyllfoot Tea Rooms in Gunnerside are located a few metres to the east of Gunnerside Bridge. Housed in an old cottage, they have the customary stone walls and beamed ceilings. The cream wallpaper is adorned with photographs of local scenes while the wooden tables are covered with floral tablecloths. The windows command a somewhat special view up Gunnerside Gill.

It is accustomed to catering for walkers, even offering a special "Hiker's Brunch" consisting of bacon, sausage, egg, black pudding, mushrooms, tomatoes, sauté potatoes, soda bread and a pot of tea. An alternative is the somewhat more daunting Ghyllfoot Grill. For anyone who is not such an ardent trencherman or woman there is Swaledale Sausage, filled Yorkshire Pudding, a Fillet of Fish, Gammon, Steak and Kidney Pie or Soup of the Day, all freshly prepared and cooked on the premises.

For the sweeter tooth the Ghyllfoot offers Fruit Cake served with a generous wedge of Swaledale Cheese, Fruit Pies and a variety of Scones including Walnut, Date, Fruit or Cheese, all delivered to the table with cholesterol-defying helpings of Jam and Cream. The large selection cakes, all home made, makes choice difficult. The same applies to the range of speciality teas and coffees.

Opening hours: Summer: daily, 10.30am to 5.30pm. (Closed Tuesdays) November-December: Week-ends only. January-February: Closed Phone 01748 886239.

Gunnerside

This compact, stone-built village with its sloping bridge spanning the Swale, dates back to Norse times, as its name implies, but reached its heyday with the lead mining boom in the eighteenth and nineteenth centuries. The lonely hillsides, which once hummed with human activity, are now lonely, almost melancholy havens for wildlife and walkers and the village is mainly dependent on agriculture and tourism.

The terrain through which this short walk passes is the haunt of several species of upland bird including curlew, lapwing, grouse, golden plover and dipper, that small, white-breasted bird to be spotted bobbing up and down on boulders in the middle of the beck.

The Route

From Gunnerside Bridge take the wide track to the east of Gunnerside Beck through the steep-sided valley. On reaching a facing white five-barred gate, turn right up a short flight of steps onto a narrower, walled path. After 20 metres negotiate a wicket gate and turn left to embark on a very gradual climb above the boulder-strewn beck.

Pass through a gated stile and continue alongside the stream, the path being extremely rocky in sections. Negotiate another stile followed immediately by a flight of stone steps to reach a footpath sign after a further 10 metres. This reads, "Gunnerside Gill, Woodland Path". Taking your direction from the arm of the post, enter Birbeck Woods, climbing to another wicket gate and continuing for a considerable distance until negotiating a stone through stile to emerge into more open country.

Turn right for 10 metres to a waymarked through stile in a stone wall and then turn left, proceeding higher into the valley along a good, grassy path. Beyond two further waymarked stiles, the valley widens and the path runs to the left of some spoil heaps and derelict buildings, the remains of a smelt mill.

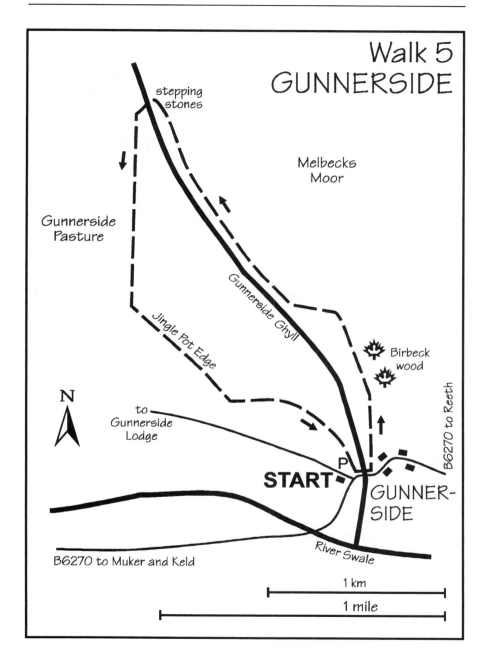

The Tea Room, Gunnerside

Just beyond, and by a waymarked boulder, turn left to the eastern bank of Gunnerside Beck. Using one of the improvised sets of stepping stones, cross to the western bank. Do not attempt to cross if the beck is in flood.

On gaining the far bank turn left along the obvious bridleway which ascends the steep slope diagonally leftwards towards Jingle Pot Edge. On the way pass to the right of a fenced-off section where serious erosion has taken place.

As you climb there is a panoramic vista up the entire length of Gunnerside Gill towards Rogan's Seat, Friarfold Moor, Great Pinseat and Great Punchard Head. On the opposite side of the valley is the bulk of Melbeck's Moor.

After approximately a kilometre of climbing, and at an altitude of 385 metres, the bridleway forms a junction with another which is heading south from Botcher Gill and the Blakethwaite lead mines. Turn left along this for a further half kilometre and, by a small cairn of stones, turn left again, this time onto a clear, turf path which loses height rapidly as it drops down the steep hillside, soon providing an aerial view of Gunnerside village.

Eventually this path swings right and passes through a very shallow valley before emerging to continue its downward course to a gated stile behind the houses. Continue a further 50 metres to the parking area by Gunnerside Beck.

Walk 6: Reeth

A gentle walk using field and riverside paths to explore the area between Reeth and Grinton.

Route: Reeth – Swing Bridge – Swale Hall – Grinton – Reeth Bridge – Reeth.

Start: The Green, Reeth. Map reference 037993.

Distance: 2½ miles (4km)

Map: "The Yorkshire Dales: Northern and Central Areas", number 30 in the O.S. "Outdoor Leisure" series.

Public Transport: Bus service number 30. Richmond – Reeth – Gunnerside. Daily except Sundays. United Bus Company.
Bus service 803. Wetherby – Leeds – Harrogate – Ripon – Leyburn – Hawes. Summer Sundays and Bank Holidays only. Harrogate and District Bus Company.
Bus service X 97. Wetherby – Leeds – Harrogate – Ripon – Reeth – Richmond. Summer Sundays and Bank Holidays only. Harrogate and District Bus Company.

By Car: Reeth is on the B6270 road between Richmond and Kirkby Stephen. There is parking around The Green. Voluntary payment of £1 is requested by the Parish Council.

The Tea Shop

Run by Richard and Caroline Duck, the Copper Kettle, occupies an old stone cottage at the lower end of The Green in Reeth. Its age is revealed by the exposed stonework and beamed ceilings although its luxuriously carpeted floor proves that it is far from spartan. The menu is designed not for ascetics but for seasoned trenchermen and women.

The Swaledale Mixed Grill includes, amongst other items, Sirloin Steak, Lamb Cutlets, Pork Gammon Steaks and local sausages. The All-Day Breakfast is of similar proportions, and is designed to keep hunger away for a week. If those two dishes sound too much like a gargantuan feast, you may fancy Roasted Ham, Steaks, Cod or a choice of sandwiches or salads.

For something in a much lighter vein, especially for the end of the

The River Swale, near Reeth

walk, there is Swaledale High Tea consisting of nothing more than sandwiches of choice, Scones with Cream and Preserves plus a portion of Yorkshire Curd Tart, all washed down with a pot of tea. People with only a meagre appetite may be satisfied with Almond Tart, Chocolate Muffin, Fruit Scone, Viennese Finger or any one of the wide selection of cakes made by Caroline. Opening times: April to September: Daily, including Sundays, 10am to 8.30pm. March and October: Daily, 10.30am to 5.30pm. November to February, inclusive, closed. Phone 01748 884748.

Reeth

The small village of Reeth occupies an important position at the junction of Arkengarthdale with Swaledale, a factor which has long made it an important centre for communications. After the granting of a market charter in 1695 it flourished for almost two centuries, its economy boosted by the rapid development of both the lead and coal mining industries in the surrounding hills. Although the market continues on Fridays, the lead mining has long since vanished with the consequence that, like other villages in Swaledale, Reeth is now largely dependent on agriculture and tourism. Its population has declined from a peak of 1,300 to a little over 300.

Testimony to its former glory as a staging post on the Richmond to Lancaster Turnpike is the large number of hotels flanking the focal point of The Green. At the lower end of this is the Swaledale Folk Museum, which shows how farming and lead mining have contributed to the shaping of the local landscape and life in this most beautiful of dales.

Grinton

The parish church of St Andrew, Grinton, is the mother church of Swaledale. Until the building of a church at Muker in the reign of Queen Elizabeth I, it served the entire valley as far away as Thwaite and Keld. Although one or two portions of the Norman building may still be seen, the present edifice dates mainly from the years between the thirteenth and fifteenth centuries. One of its more unusual features is the "Leper's Squint", a slit in the stonework which allowed the afflicted to observe the Mass while remaining isolated from the remainder of the congregation.

Until the building of the church at Muker, the dead were carried to Grinton from as far afield as Keld, using what became known as "The

Corpse Road", portions of which have been incorporated into some of the routes in this collection.

Grinton Bridge was designed by the celebrated York Architect, John Carr, who was also responsible for the design of Harewood House. Built in 1797 as part of the turnpiking of the roads, it replaced an earlier one which, according to the mid-sixteenth-century traveller, John Leland, was "a fair bridge".

The Route

Leave The Green by the south-west corner, passing Barclay's Bank on the way. Turn right and, by the far end of "Freal House", bear left into an alleyway or 'Ginnel' signed "To The River". This leads to a road through a small housing estate. Turn left along this road for 70 metres to a T-junction where there is a footpath sign to Swing Bridge.

By this sign turn right along Quaker Lane which once provided access to a Quaker School endowed by Leonard Raw in the late eighteenth century. This has long since vanished, its site now occupied by a house, but its successor may be seen on the flank of the hill to the north. Quaker Lane provides a fine view up Swaledale while to the left, on the far side of the River Swale, stands Harkerside Moor.

Where Quaker Lane reaches two facing green metal five-barred gates, turn left into a sunken lane to pass through a wooden five-barred gate adjacent to a field barn before maintaining direction to a small wooden footbridge. From the far end swing right along the clear path, pass through a derelict hedgerow and cross the riverside pasture to a small wooden gate. Continue for a further 20 metres while staying to the left of some sheep pens then make a left turn over the Swing Bridge spanning the River Swale. At the far end, turn left again, taking a bearing on a solitary hawthorn tree standing by a bend in the river where noisy oystercatchers frequent the large shingle beds in early Spring.

Where the path meets a Y-junction turn left through a gateway with a redundant stile adjacent and stay forward between the River Swale on your left and a wire fence on your right to reach a small wooden gate. Maintain the same line of direction while staying to the right of a barbed wire fence to a wooden five-barred gate in a field corner.

Turn left through this and, within 5 metres, negotiate a squeezer stile to join the tree-lined Low Lane, believed to be one of the oldest thoroughfares in the Yorkshire Dales. As the river has curved well away to the left at this point, climb slightly to pass a field barn on your right and a row of dead trees on your left. Running up the valley at right

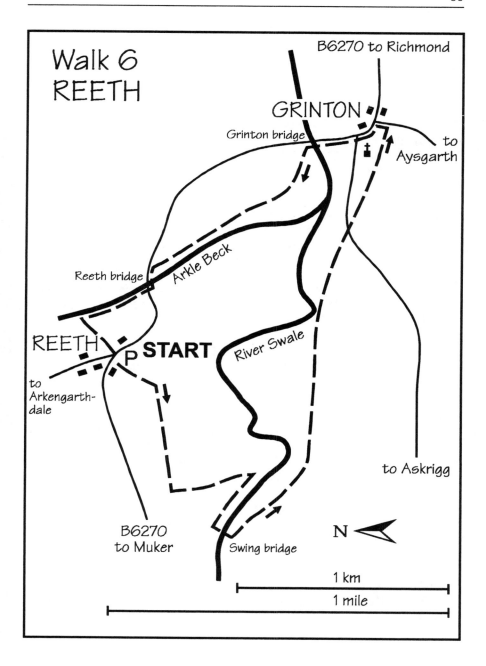

Walk 6
REETH

B6270 to Richmond

GRINTON

Grinton bridge

to Aysgarth

Arkle Beck

Reeth bridge

REETH

P START

to Arkengarth-dale

River Swale

B6270 to Muker

Swing bridge

to Askrigg

N

1 km

1 mile

angles to Low Lane, is an earth embankment with a ditch in front of it. This is thought to be either the remains of a Romano-British defensive structure or the remnants of a medieval deer barrier.

A short distance beyond this point Low Lane becomes walled, passes through two small wooden gates and reaches one of the metal five-barred variety. Some 10 metres beyond this it forms a junction with the minor surfaced road which runs through Harkerside to Wensleydale. A short distance to your right, on slightly higher ground, stands Swale Hall, an impressive edifice once the home of an important local family.

Turn left along the road in the direction of Grinton but, on the first bend, turn right through a gated stile. After 10 metres bear left through a small gate and, keeping two small hummocks on your right, reach a squeezer stile adjacent to some farm outbuildings, a mixture of stone and green corrugated metal.

Cross the next field directly to a squeezer stile and then bear left over a flagged footbridge spanning a stream before following the clear path to another small wooden gate in the left-hand field corner.

Through that turn left down a short lane to join the Askrigg road. Turn left again along this for a few metres to meet the B6270 by Grinton Church and opposite the Bridge Inn.

Turn left along the main road in the direction of Reeth. Cross Grinton Bridge and, at the far end, make a turn through a wicket gate on your left to descend a short flight of stone steps onto the distinct path heading away from the river towards a conspicuous kissing gate with a footpath sign adjacent.

From the kissing gate bear right towards a field corner and take a bearing on the farm ahead. Keep the barns on your right, walking between them and Arkle Beck to another wicket gate and continuing beyond a footpath sign to rendezvous with the B6270 again. Using the pavement, turn left in the direction of Reeth. Be extra vigilant in crossing Reeth Bridge.

Over the bridge and by a footpath sign make an immediate turn left onto "Beckside Walk". Initially, pass through a gap between the end of a wall and a fence. Then turn left as the path doubles back on itself to pass under the bridge. From this point onwards it partners Arkle Beck which is on your right.

Ignore the first footpath sign and stile, continuing forward to "Arkle Cottage". By this bear left to meet a surfaced road and another footpath sign. Turn left for the short climb onto The Green in the centre of Reeth.

Walk 7: Richmond

Designed to link the secular with the spiritual aspects of medieval Yorkshire, this gentle route provides several glimpses into the past.

Route: Richmond – Anchorage Hill – Easby Abbey – St Agatha's Church – Railway Bridge – Richmond.

Start: The car park, Victoria Road, Richmond. Map reference 168011.

Distance: 3¼ miles (5 km)

Map: "Richmond and Leyburn", number 609 in the O.S. "Pathfinder" series.

Public Transport: Richmond is served by daily buses from Darlington which is on the main East Coast railway line. National Express (Phone: 01990 808080).
United Bus Company operates local bus services from Richmond to Swaledale, Coverdale, Wensleydale and other nearby towns.

By Car: Richmond is linked to the Al at Scotch Corner by the A6108. From the west leave the M6 at Junction 37 to follow the A684 through Sedbergh to Hawes and Leyburn and then the A6108 to Richmond. There are several car parks in the town. The one in Victoria Road is Long Stay and Pay and Display.

The Tea Shop

Richmond has a wealth of tea shops and cafés from which to choose but the Richmond Bakery in Queen's Road has the advantage of being close to the Victoria car park. In its own way it has managed to encapsulate the feel and atmosphere of this ancient and historic town.

The beamed ceiling is matched by white upper walls which are partnered by a floral wainscot and an ancient dresser. The old York fireplace, still cleaned with black lead, is topped by potted palms and oil lamps while prints and photographs adorn the walls. The tables are covered with lace cloths and surrounded by spindle-backed chairs.

The very basis of the menu is bread, baked on the premises and amongst the finest to be found, not only in Yorkshire, but anywhere in the world. This explains the enormous sandwich menu and the "Richmond Bombs". These are large bread rolls with a choice of fillings such as Coronation Chicken or Chicken Tikka. Other substantial dishes on offer include the Dalesman Cheese Platter, composed of a selection of local cheeses, freshly-dressed Whitby Crab or Soup of the Day.

For the end of the walk or that mid-afternoon break there is an equally bewildering array of freshly baked scones including Fruit, Wholemeal, Date or Cheese, all served with gargantuan helpings of Jam and Cream. The Richmond Cream Tea is a speciality of the house as is the Apple and Cinnamon Torte, oozing its filling of apples, sultanas and spices and served with a generous slice of Wensleydale or Swaledale Cheese. Another highlight is the Quivering Caramel Cheesecake but there is a display of other mouth-watering cakes and gateaux from which to choose.

To accompany all these meals, large or small, there is an extensive range of speciality teas and coffees. Afterwards, passing through the shop, you may purchase any of the teas, coffees, bread, scones or cakes that you have sampled – or not sampled – in the tea room. Opening times: All year, Monday to Saturday. 8.30am to 5pm. Closed Sundays. Phone 01748 850625.

Richmond

Stand in the Richmond's Market Square and you will immediately experience the history firmly embedded in its stones. Yet, despite this atmosphere, the town did not exist prior to the Norman Conquest. Indeed, it did not even rate a mention in that national survey of 1086, the Domesday Book.

It owes its origins to the Castle, built as the focal point of a new Bastide or fortified town, created by the Normans shortly after they had subjected the rebellious North of England. Its strategic purpose was to over-awe the Saxons and was of such a size and strength that it succeeded admirably without experiencing much in the way of military action. In course of time it held two Scottish kings as prisoners, William the Lion in 1174 and David II in 1346, both having been defeated in battle by the English. At the end of the Civil War in England, Charles 1 lodged there on his journey south in 1647.

The "new" town was carefully planned at the same time as the Castle, being designed on the then Continental style with several narrow wynds leading into the Market Square which is the largest in England. Standing on an island in the centre of the Square is Trinity Church, unique in that it has shops in its disused north aisle. Today it houses the Museum of the Green Howards, the local regiment, which was opened in 1973 by King Olaf of Norway, the Commander-in-Chief.

The original Market Cross was demolished in 1771 to be replaced by the present Obelisk. Grey Friars Tower in Friary Gardens is the main surviving relic of the Franciscan Friary which occupied the site until the Reformation.

One of the jewels in Richmond's crown is the Georgian Theatre Royal where the curtain first rose in 1788 and where plays, operas and concerts are still staged by professional companies. Among the famous stars who have trodden its boards are Edmund Kean, Sarah Siddons, Ellen Tree and Keith Michell.

Yorkshire's Richmond gave its name to the town in Surrey and several other Richmonds around the world, especially in the United States of America. The Yorkshire town is very scornful of its Surrey namesake's claim to the celebrated song, "The Lass of Richmond Hill". Local historians have dug deep into the records to identify her as a Yorkshire lass. Details of all these and the town's other attractions may be obtained from the Tourist Information Centre, Victoria Road, Richmond, North Yorkshire. DL10 4AJ. Phone: 01748 850252.

Easby Abbey

Founded in 1152, Easby Abbey, dedicated to St Agatha, belonged to the Premonstratensian Order, or White Canons as they were known from

Easby Abbey

the colour of their habits. In comparison with the other great ecclesiastical institutions of the Dales – Fountains, Jervaulx and Bolton – Easby was a comparatively minor establishment but still sufficiently wealthy to attract the attentions of the marauding Scots on their frequent raids south of the Border. In 1346 an English army, on its way to do battle with the Scots at Neville's Cross, was billeted within the abbey precincts. As a result of their drunken brawls they inflicted considerable damage and the monks were only too pleased to see their 'protectors' depart. Afterwards it was restored only to succumb to the greed of Henry VIII at the time of the Reformation.

Adjacent stands Easby Parish Church, also dedicated to St Agatha. Surprisingly it pre-dates the monastic foundation. Portions of the original building have been incorporated into the present building which is in the Early English style. It contains some fine, well preserved murals depicting scenes from both the Old and New Testaments. There is also a plaster replica of the Easby Cross, the original of which, dating from the seventh century, is preserved in the Victoria and Albert Museum in London.

Easby Abbey is in the care of English Heritage. Opening times: 22nd March to 31st October: Daily, 10.00am to 6.00pm. There is an entry charge.

The Route

Leave the car park by turning left along Victoria Road and, immediately before the Theatre Royal, turning right into Friars' Wynd to reach the Market Square facing the Obelisk and Trinity Church. Turn left by the shops. At the bottom of the Square, make another left turn into Frenchgate. Continue downhill but, by the first corner of the Richmondshire District Council Offices, make a right turn into a narrow alleyway.

Descend a flight of steps and, after 100 metres, fork left at a Y-junction to pass through a wall gap before continuing to swing round to the left while passing to the right of some tennis courts and Richmond School. By an obvious millstone fork right towards the River Swale to pass beneath Mercury Bridge on a riverside path. 100 metres beyond, and facing a wall, go left to pass to the right of a stone house to reach a T-junction.

Turn right along the broad track signed to Easby Abbey. Initially this climbs slightly and gently above the Swale to enter the woodlands clothing the slope of Anchorage Hill. Through the gaps between the trees there are some fine views of Richmond Castle away to your right.

At the next junction, by the grounds of "The Boat House", fork left

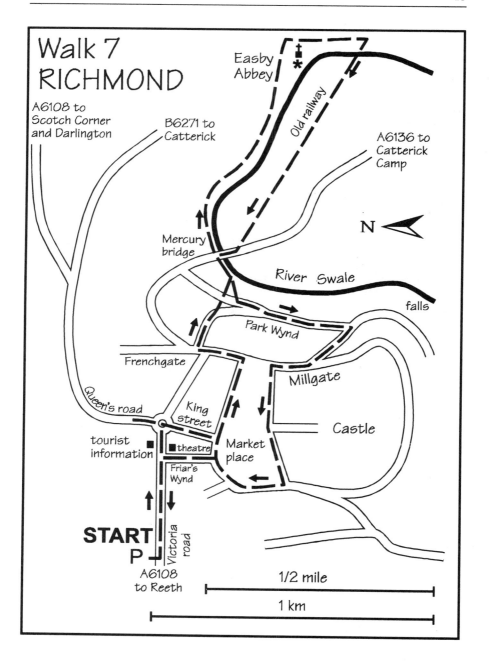

Walk 7
RICHMOND

A6108 to
Scotch Corner
and Darlington

B6271 to
Catterick

Easby
Abbey

Old railway

A6136 to
Catterick
Camp

N

Mercury
bridge

River Swale

falls

Park Wynd

Frenchgate

Millgate

Queen's road

King
street

Castle

tourist
information

theatre

Market
place

Friar's
Wynd

Victoria road

START
P

A6108
to Reeth

1/2 mile

1 km

along the fenced path, leaving the woodlands and moving further away from the river. Pass to the left of a solitary house and continue forward until another path comes in from the right immediately before a wooden stile.

Turn left over the stile and then immediately left again over a second to follow a diversion instituted because the original path has been washed away by the river. Over the second stile turn right, crossing the field diagonally to a stile by a solitary tree and in front of the impressive-looking St Agatha's House, the former Vicarage of Easby Parish Church. Over this stile maintain your direction on a clear, distinctive path to a telegraph pole where a swing to the left leads to another stile. Over this turn right, as directed by a waymark, to follow the driveway of St Agatha's House for approximately 100 metres to meet a minor road. Turn right, descending the slope to the car park serving both Easby Abbey and the parish church of St Agatha. By this car park, where the surfaced road terminates, fork left along a wide track but, just before "Platelayer's Cottage", make a right turn onto a former railway bridge with white railings and cross the River Swale.

Continue along the track of the railway until, having passed the site of the former station and the Sports Centre, emerge onto the A6136 on the outskirts of Richmond.

Turn right over Mercury Bridge, known as Station Bridge until it was re-named in 1975 to mark the 50th anniversary of the Royal Corps of Signals being stationed at nearby Catterick Camp.

50 metres beyond the far end of the bridge turn left onto the riverside path which formed a stretch of the outward route. However, this time stay close to the wall on the right as it curves round but, by the same millstone and green benches, fork left into Park Wynd to climb with a view of the Richmond Falls away to your left.

Where the track joins Riverside Road bear left for 10 metres to the junction with Millgate. Turn right to climb more steeply towards the Castle which is directly ahead. On reaching the Market Square walk round before turning left into King Street and, at the far end and by the traffic island, staying forward into Queen's Road for the Tea Shop. Afterwards, retrace your steps to the traffic island and turn right into Victoria Road for the car park.

Walk 8: Hardraw

An easy stroll through pastures typical of the landscape of the Dales.

Route: Hardraw – Simonstone – Sedbusk – Haylands Bridge – Hardraw.

Start: The Craft Shop opposite the Green Dragon Inn, Hardraw village. Map reference, 867913.

Distance: 2½ miles (4km)

Map: "The Yorkshire Dales: Northern and Central Areas", number 30 in the O.S. "Outdoor Leisure" series.

Public Transport: None.

By Car: Hardraw may be reached by the minor road from Hawes signed to Sedbusk, Hardraw and Muker. At the T-junction beyond Haylands Bridge turn left for Hardraw. There are several parking spots in the village and the Parish Council requests a small donation from motorists towards the cost of maintaining the parish church.

The Tea Shop

The name "Hardraw", apparently has developed from the early English for "Shepherd's Dwelling", which is somewhat appropriate considering that the village was once a far-flung grange owned by the monks of Fountains Abbey who used the surrounding hills for rearing sheep. Not surprisingly, directly opposite to the Green Dragon Inn, there stands the Shepherd's Kitchen Cafe and Craft Shop. It occupies the pub's former coach house. With its wooden beams, check gingham curtains, large stone fireplace, ornamental tea pots, wooden tables and brass and copperware ornaments, it offers welcome hospitality to all who enter through its doors.

Barbara Thwaite offers a feast of treats including her three-layered Chocolate and Coffee Cakes, Fruit Cake served with a slice of Wensleydale Cheese and Scones, fresh from the Aga, smothered in Jam and Cream. Her Yorkshire Cream Tea is one of the wonders of the Dales. For that more substantial repast there is a selection of dishes ranging from Soup of the Day to Savoury Sausage Slice and the Dales Shepherd's

Platter. In addition to Horlicks and milk there is a choice of both speciality teas and coffees.

Opening hours: April to October: Daily 10.00am to 6.00pm. November to March. Saturdays and Sundays only. 10.00am to 6.00pm. Phone 01969 667679.

Hardraw

Hardraw, little more than a hamlet a short distance to the north of Hawes, is noted for its famous waterfall, Hardraw Force, which plunges dramatically for 30 metres (100 feet) into the basin of a natural rock amphitheatre. This makes it the highest waterfall above ground in England. By the approach path there is a circular stone bandstand where the Hardraw Brass Band Contest is staged every September, still attracting premier bands from all parts of the United Kingdom as it has done since 1881.

The celebrated French tightrope walker, Blondin, crossed over the fall before his much more publicised feat of crossing the Niagara Falls. Turner, the famous landscape painter, captured Hardraw on canvas during his tour of the North of England.

The Force may only be reached through the Green Dragon Inn, one of the oldest watering holes in the Yorkshire Dales. There is recorded evidence to prove that it occupied the same location in the early sixteenth century while there is a

Hardraw Force

probability that there was a hostelry on the site even 300 years before that.

It appears to have been established initially as a grange or lodging house for the lay brothers of Fountains Abbey when they visited the area to hold checks on their flocks of sheep in the district.

The unusual name does not indicate the existence of some fierce creature in days gone by but refers to the green dragon to be found on the flag or standard that was raised in Hardraw as a rallying point for local men reporting for their forty days of liege service to their lord during feudal times.

The Route

From the "Shepherd's Kitchen" cross the road to the Green Dragon and, passing to the right-hand side of the pub, turn right through a small wooden gate onto a path signed to Simonstone. Pass behind a cottage for 10 metres to a second wooden gate before following the flagged path to the right of a wall. Beyond a stile the path, still flagged, continues with a wall on the left. Where this bends away slightly, bear right up the slope towards a small wooden enclosure as the flags give way to cobbles. At this point the cascading waters of Hardraw Force are clearly audible but invisible a short distance away to your left.

Beyond the enclosure climb steeply for 100 metres to a wooden stile and walk to the left of "West House". Below is a splendid view of the houses of Hardraw huddled closely together.

By the corner of "West House" turn right to a gated stile by a metal five-barred gate. Pass between the house on your right and a set of outbuildings on your left before taking the obvious path over the next field.

Having negotiated another gated stile proceed to the right of the boundary wall of Simonstone Hall, now a hotel. Directly in front of the Hall turn left through a stile and then immediately right, as directed by a waymark. Proceed along the unsurfaced driveway for 100 metres to meet the road from Hawes to Muker in Swaledale.

Make a left turn along the road for some 15 metres and then turn right through a gated stile by a footpath sign indicating a path to Sedbusk.

Initially follow a broad track which goes to the left of some farm outbuildings, and then negotiate a ladder stile by a set of metal double five-barred gates. Using the clear path, maintain the same line of direction to cross a succession of narrow fields by a series of stiles.

When the village of Sedbusk comes into view but a short distance ahead, negotiate a gated stile by a pylon and advance over the next narrow field to a squeezer stile. Through that, turn diagonally right to a gated stile alongside a footpath finger post and a metal five-barred gate. This provides access into Sedbusk Lane.

Turn right for 15 metres and, by another footpath sign, turn left through a gated stile. Descend the slope while staying to the right of a barn and enjoying superb views of Wether Fell, Addleborough and Upper Wensleydale.

Beyond the first gated stone step stile climb for approximately 50 metres to a small gate and follow the clear, serpentine path over a sloping field. Finally lose altitude to a junction of paths by yet another gated stile.

This provides an exit onto the Hawes to Bainbridge road. Cross this,

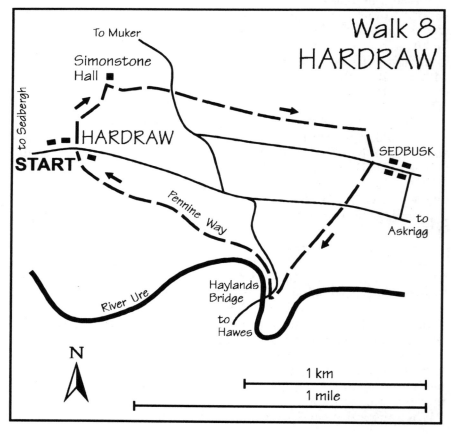

bearing slightly right to a gated stile with a sign to Haylands Bridge adjacent.

Heading towards the River Ure, follow the path across a large meadow before negotiating a gated squeezer stile and crossing a stone-arched and cobbled pack horse bridge. From the far end of this maintain direction to another stile and Brunt Acres Road, a few metres to the north of Haylands Bridge.

Turn right. Ignore the first path on the left, which crosses a football pitch. Proceed along the road for a further 150 metres. There turn left up a short flight of stone steps and pass through a wooden gate to join the signed Pennine Way. This follows its obvious course through another succession of gated stiles until emerging by the "Shepherd's Kitchen" in Hardraw.

Walk 9: Hawes

Another exploration of the rich pastoral landscape of Upper Wensleydale, mainly using field paths and lanes.

Route: Hawes – Bainbridge Ings – Burtersett – Shaw Lane – Gayle – Hawes.

Distance: 3¾ miles (5.8 km)

Start: The National Park car park, Station Yard, Hawes. Map reference, 876899.

Map: "The Yorkshire Dales: Northern and Central Areas", number 30 in the O.S. "Outdoor Leisure" series.

Public Transport: Garsdale Station on the Settle-Carlisle line is connected to Hawes by bus on summer Tuesdays, Fridays and Sundays.
Dalesbus service 800. Leeds – Bradford – Ilkley – Hawes. Tuesdays, Saturdays and Sundays during late July and August. Keighley and District Bus Co.
Dalesbus services 804 and 805. Leeds – Bradford – Keighley – Skipton – Hawes. Summer Sundays only. Keighley and District Bus Co.
Postbus Service: Northallerton – Bedale – Leyburn – Hawes. Mondays to Saturdays all year. Services 26 and 142: Richmond – Leyburn – Hawes. Several daily, Mondays to Saturdays. United Bus Co.

By Car: Hawes is situated on the A684 Sedbergh to Leyburn road. It may also be reached by minor roads from Kettlewell, Ingleton and Muker.

The Tea Shop

Located on the Aysgarth road, close to the National Park car park, Beckindales Tea Room is conveniently situated for the end of this walk. With its raised gallery, hand-carved wooden tables and chairs, walls decorated with sickles, cross-saws and hay forks, it provides a pleasant environment in which to relax after your walk. There is also a display of crafts and speciality preserves for sale.

If you have worked-up a substantial appetite there is Whitby Seafood Platter, Scampi and Chips, Lasagne, Bacon and Eggs, Steak Pie or

Wensleydale Ploughman's to choose from. Scones, baked on the premises, come in three forms – plain, fruit or cheese – all served with a superfluity of cream and home-made preserves. Fruit Loaf is accompanied by a wedge of locally-made Wensleydale Cheese as is the Apple Pie. Other cakes include Apple Danish, Cherry Pie, Apricot Crumble smothered in cream, Date and Walnut Cake, Carrot Cake or American Blueberry Muffin. There is, as you would expect, an extensive range of coffees and teas in addition to soft drinks. Opening times: Daily, 10.30am to 5pm. Closed January and Fridays November to March.

Hawes

Standing at 850 feet above sea level, Hawes claims to be the highest market town in England. Surrounded on three sides by high moorlands, it is a busy, bustling place serving the whole of Upper Wensleydale. It is also at the centre of a network of roads. One heads south through Widdale to Ingleton and Settle, another crosses Garsdale Head to Sedbergh and Kendal while a third climbs over the Buttertubs Pass to Muker and Swaledale. Two roads, one north of the River Ure and one to the south, the A684, link it with Leyburn.

Gayle

Yet, until as recently as 1699, when it was granted a market charter, it was very much inferior to Gayle. Its rising prosperity was accentuated by the building of the Turnpike Road with the resulting clutch of coaching inns, many of which still survive.

Hawes is probably most famous as the home of Wensleydale Cheese. Originally manufactured from ewe's milk by the monks of Jervaulx Abbey, and later by farmers' wives, the present creamery in Gayle Lane was opened in 1897. After a financial crisis it was rescued through the efforts of the legendary Kit Calvert and, after a successful spell, was acquired by Dairy Crest. Their recent plans to close it down and transfer production to Lancashire was the final insult and almost led to another War of the Roses. This tragedy was averted by a management buy-out and today the Hawes Creamery is thriving with its production of hand-made cheeses and extending varieties. In 1992 a new Visitor Centre was opened so that it is now possible to see the cheese being produced. It is the latest visitor attraction in the dale. Another attraction for visitors is Outhwaites, the Ropemakers, which is located by the car park. The Dales Countryside Museum, with its fascinating displays of life and work in the Dales, is an absolute must for all who really wish to understand this fine walking region.

The Route

Exit the car park by turning left and, at the first road junction, make another left turn along the Aysgarth road, the A684. Pass Hawes Cattle Market on your right and, by a footpath finger post approximately 15 metres before reaching the Wensleydale Press, also on your right, make a right turn through a small wooden gate to follow a flagged path. Climb gradually across the field to a squeezer stile before continuing a further 10 metres to another footpath sign and a gated stile. This permits access onto the minor road leading from the A684 to Gayle.Cross this road diagonally to the left, a distance of about 10 metres. Climb a flight of 4 stone steps adjacent to a footpath sign reading, "Burtersett ¾ miles", and negotiate a gated stile to enter an area of land known as Bainbridge Ings. The path bears diagonally left to a gated stile a short distance to the right of a pylon. Beyond, maintain the same line of direction to a stile alongside a barn. Remain forward to the left of a field barn before curving round to the right to another stile from where there is a fine prospect of the whole of Upper Wensleydale. Continue through two more gated stiles and then aim for a metal five-barred gate in the facing wall. However, *do not use this*. Instead, a few metres before reaching it,

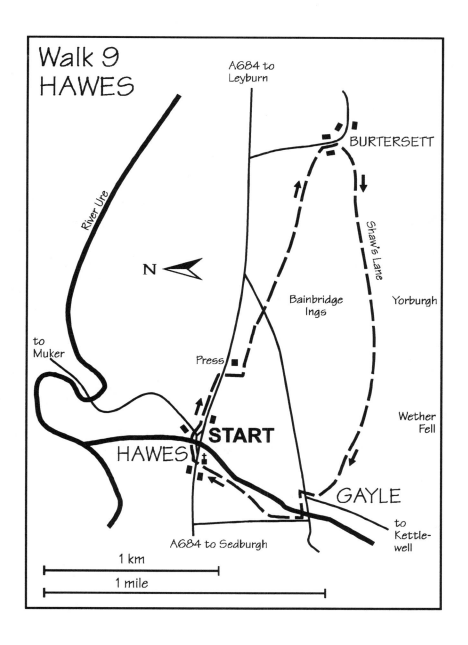

Walk 9
HAWES

A684 to
Leyburn

River Ure

BURTERSETT

N

Shaw's Lane

Bainbridge
Ings

Yorburgh

to
Muker

Press

Wether
Fell

START

HAWES

GAYLE

A684 to Sedburgh

to
Kettle-
well

1 km

1 mile

bend round further towards the right before staying with the well-trodden path which climbs gradually to a through stile in the wall on the
left. Cross the next field by veering very slightly towards the right while
heading for another obvious gated stile.

Cross the centre of the next field to a small wicket gate by the
conspicuous white gable-end of the Wesleyan Church.

Pass between the Church on your right and a large house on your left
to reach the minor road through Burtersett. Turn right but, at the
Y-junction after 100 metres, bear right to pass "South View" house
before reaching a two-armed finger post. Ignore the path signed to
Wether Fell, choosing to remain forward into Shaws Lane which is
signed to Gayle.

This walled lane commands views along the valley towards Garsdale
Head while Wether Fell at 614 metres and Yorburgh reaching 515
metres, dominate the skyline to your left. Great Shunner fell is visible
to the right.

On reaching a wooden five-barred gate pass through the gated stile
adjacent. From this point the track is walled only on the left. Pass to the
left of a large barn before bearing slightly right to a gated stile by a metal
five-barred gate and then veering left to a squeezer stile. Remain to the
left of another field barn to a stile and then advance to the right of a
barn to reach a stile with a footpath finger post alongside.

Continue along the same bearing to the next stile, alongside a metal
five-barred gate and also with a footpath finger post. From there aim for
the three-armed finger post ahead.

Select the somewhat indistinct path to the left of a barn which is
signed "Gayle South" and leads to an obvious ladder stile. Over this
maintain the same line of direction to a stone step stile, another ladder
stile and a stone step stile 15 metres to the right of a five-barred gate
with blue-capped gateposts.

Stay forward to the next step stile and then draw closer to the wall
on the right. Follow this round to a small wooden gate in the right-hand
corner of the field, ignoring another small gate adjacent to a five-barred
one.

Through the appropriate gate stay to the left of a wall to a stile which
is a peculiar combination of the through and stone- step varieties.
Beyond, curve left to a wall corner and then lose altitude until meeting
the road from Hawes to Kettlewell.

Turn right to enter the village of Gayle with the beck flowing in from
the left. At the first Y-junction fork left over the stone bridge but, at the

next junction, turn right in the direction of Hawes. After approximately 200 metres beyond the last house on the right, turn right onto a paved path signed as a section of the Pennine Way. Follow this as it passes to the right of the Wensleydale Creamery and to the left of Hawes parish church to emerge onto the A684 by a bend in the centre of Hawes.

Follow the A684 in the direction of Aysgarth and, having passed the entrance to the Muker road turn left to regain the car park or stay forward a few metres to Beckindales and that well-earned cuppa and cake.

Walk 10: Aysgarth

A pastoral route in central Wensleydale and into the lower reaches of Bishopdale.

Route: Aysgarth Falls – Aysgarth Church – Eshington Bridge – Eastfield Lane – Thoralby – Folly Lane – Aysgarth – Aysgarth Falls.

Start: The National Park car park, Aysgarth Falls. Map reference 012887.

Distance: 5 miles (8km)

Map: "The Yorkshire Dales: Northern and Central Areas" number 30 in the O.S. "Outdoor Leisure" series.

Public Transport: Service 156. Richmond – Leyburn – Aysgarth – Hawes. United Bus Co.
Dalesbus service 800. Leeds – Bradford – Ilkley – Aysgarth – Hawes. Tuesdays late July and August and summer Saturdays and Sundays. Keighley and District Bus Co.
Postbus: Northallerton – Bedale – Leyburn – Aysgarth – Hawes. Mondays to Saturdays all year.

By Car: The National Park car park at Aysgarth Falls is signed from the A684 Leyburn to Hawes road, a short distance east of Aysgarth village. The Pay and Display car park is the converted station yard adjacent to the minor road linking the A684 with Carperby.

The Tea Shop

The Mill Race Tea Shop, overlooking the celebrated Aysgarth Falls, once formed part of the Yore Mill, built in 1784 by the Birbeck family. It stands next to the Yorkshire Carriage Museum. Its antiquity is revealed in the thick, colour-washed stone walls and massive oak beams. The Mill Race is proud of its own bakery which is housed in the cellar and allows the proprietors, Allan Hopkins and his wife, to produce not only their own cakes but also the other dishes on the menu. In addition they sell their own selection of "Mill Race" preserves and pickles as well as other local produce.

Speciality teas include Earl Grey, Darjeeling, Assam and Ceylon in addition to various Herbals and Fruit. Coffee addicts may order a

The Mill Race Tea Shop

cafetière of Brazilian High Roast, House Blend or Medium. There is also a choice of soft drinks, milk shakes and Coca-Cola.

Light lunches feature Wensleydale Cheese with Celery sticks and rough Oatcakes, Minestrone Soup, Sausage Pie and a whole range of toasted sandwiches. Main course lunches offer Yorkshire Ham Salad, hot Sausage Pie, Wensleydale Cheese Ploughman's based on Blue, Smoked or plain Wensleydale Cheese or a fresh Whitby Crab Salad.

For that tea-time treat there are Toasted Teacakes smothered in jam, Heart-Shaped Waffles oozing Maple Syrup and topped with Cream, Sticky Ginger Parkin, Yorkshire Fat Rascals – fruit drop scones – Rich Fruit Cake accompanied by a wedge of Wensleydale Cheese and a slice of apple and a selection of home-made cakes fresh from the cellar. The Aysgarth Special Tea starts with Salmon and Cucumber sandwiches followed by Scones, strawberry jam, cream and a choice of either tea or coffee. Opening times: Easter to 31st October: 10.30am to 5.00pm. November, February and March: open week-ends only. Christmas holiday period: daily 11.00am to dusk. Phone 01969 663446.

Aysgarth

Aysgarth appears in Domesday Book as "Eshescard", which apparently translates as "an open space marked by oaks". It is perhaps most famous for its series of three waterfalls which attract visitors from all parts of the world. The Yore Mill, dating from 1784 and now housing the Yorkshire Carriage Museum, has produced both flour and cloth. During the Wars of Italian Unification in the nineteenth century, it was responsible for clothing the soldiers of Garibaldi's army in their distinctive red flannel. The parish church of St Andrew occupies an ancient religious site. A tenth-century stone cross, discovered in 1968 in a wall near the churchyard, was placed on display inside the church. Sadly, it was stolen in 1996. The first church was built on the site in the late twelfth century, although most of the present edifice dates from the nineteenth. The most notable feature of St Andrew's is the early sixteenth-century Rood Screen, which was removed from nearby Jervaulx Abbey at the time of the Dissolution of the Monasteries.

The Route

Leave the car park by taking the footpath in the south-west corner signed "Upper Falls". Where this meets the road from Carperby to Aysgarth, continue forward across the road bridge with a fine view of the Upper Falls on your right. At the far end of the bridge leave the road by maintaining the same direction and keeping to the right of the Carriage Museum before climbing the stepped path to St Andrew's Church.

Corner the East End of the church before resuming your original direction through the churchyard to enter the walled Vicarage Lane which leads to the A684. Cross directly to the gated stile by the footpath sign which indicates a route to Eshington Bridge.

Descend the grassy slope to another sign and a wooden stile and then climb alongside a wire fence on your left to a small wicket gate. Continue to the immediate right of a stone wall to a finger post on the crest of the hill. By this turn right, as indicated, to a waymarked gate.

Stay forward to the left of a wall corner and then bend towards the left to reach a gate and another footpath sign in the field corner. Advance a further 20 metres, as suggested by the waymark to a footpath sign. By this turn left through a gated stile and aim some 20 metres to the left of a pylon. Here a gated stile provides an exit onto the Aysgarth to

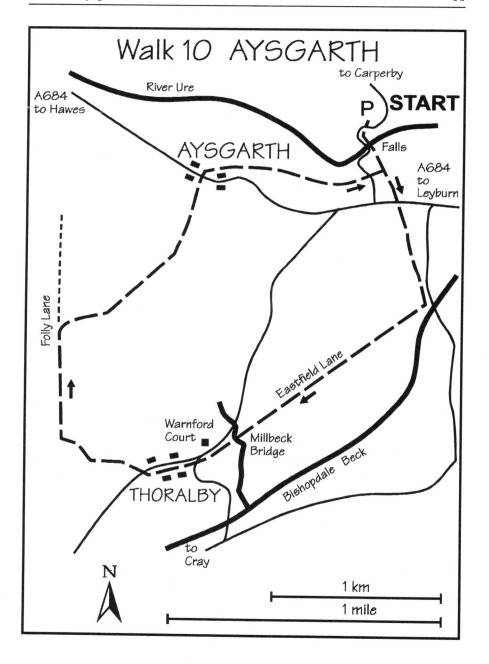

Walk 10 AYSGARTH

to Carperby

P START

River Ure

A684
to Hawes

AYSGARTH

Falls

A684
to
Leyburn

Folly Lane

Eastfield Lane

Warnford
Court

Millbeck
Bridge

Bishopdale Beck

THORALBY

to
Cray

N

1 km

1 mile

Kettlewell road by its junction with Eastfield Lane. A few metres ahead the road bends left over Eshington Bridge which spans Bishopdale Beck.

Immediately through the stile ignore the road. Instead make a right turn into Eastfield Lane which runs parallel to Bishopdale Beck. The length of the delightful Bishopdale lies ahead, its flanks guarded on the south by Burton Moor and Harland Hill.

Beyond Spickels Farms the lane loses its metalled surface and, shortly after crossing the moss-festooned Millbeck Bridge, reaches a minor road. Turn left to enter the village of Thoralby with the impressive-looking Heaning Hall, now a farm, set back a short distance from the road. Closer to the village, and also on the right, is the equally imposing Warnford Court.

Thoralby boasts a number of fascinating old stone cottages. What history, for instance, is secreted within the walls of "Lingdale"? It carries a plaque reading: "J & R.W. 1811"

Another with an even longer pedigree stands opposite "The Grange". The lintel above the door carries the legend, "1653. I. B." The Old Chapel House and the former Methodist Church are now both private residences.

Saunter along the village street absorbing these intriguing facets of Dales history but, by the Post Office and the Village Green bear right, moving away from the main road to pass "The George Inn". Opposite "Kenley Cottage" make a right turn into Haw Lane to reach a footpath finger post after 20 metres. This indicates routes to Bell Busk and Aysgarth.

Follow this wide, walled lane as it climbs steeply and bends left to offer a stupendous vista of Upper Bishopdale and the dark, rolling moorlands beyond which separate it from Upper Wharfedale.

After a considerable distance Haw Lane bends sharply to the right, reaching a metal five-barred gate. Proceed through this and continue climbing to the left of a wall until the main track turns sharply left at Keld Gill. Stay forward for a few metres to a gated stile adjacent to a metal five-barred gate with a bridleway sign.

Taking your direction from the arm of the sign, fork right across the grass to a waymarker in a collapsed drystone wall and then maintain your direction over the turf to a waymarked small wooden gate in the right-hand corner of the field. Through that, advance to the left of a wall and descend to a wicket gate which provides entry into a walled lane.

Immediately ford a stream by utilising the carefully arranged stones and embark on the first short climb along Folly Lane. As it levels, it acquires a grassy surface which provides both comfort for the feet and pleasant easy walking.

50 metres before reaching Folly House barn, and by a footpath sign, turn right through a gated stile onto a field path which initially clings closely to the wall on the right before gradually moving across the field. Approximately 30 metres before the left-hand corner of the field, and by a footpath sign, turn left through a wall gap and head diagonally right for 50 metres to a gated stile.

Beyond that, veer left to the far corner of the next field and a through stile on the right. Stay forward a few metres to a wooden stile in a new wire fence. Then veer left to pass through a gateway adjacent to the right-side of a barn.

Continue along the same line of direction, crossing the field diagonally to pass through another wall gap to a gated stile. From there aim for a wooden electricity pylon with an adjacent through stile. Cross the next field to a gated stile close by the corner.

Take direction from the overhead wires, while staying close to a wall on your right to negotiate a very well constructed through stile. Advance to a similar one after 50 metres and then bear left to a stile in the facing wall, passing to the right of a field barn on the way. On the far side of the wall make a left turn to a through stile by a metal five-barred gate which allows entry to a lane.

Stay with this as it runs to the left of a wall. Pass through a gateway but, where the track curves left, maintain direction over the grass and close to the wall on your right. Beyond a gated stile pass between the houses to meet a minor road on the outskirts of Aysgarth village.

Turn right for 30 metres to the A684. Turn right in the direction of Leyburn. After approximately 150 metres where the road bears right and by the War Memorial, leave the main road by staying forward to pass the Methodist Church. By the house, "Calf Garth" and a footpath sign, bend right to a gated stile alongside a metal five-barred gate.

Remain to the left of the wall for about 40 metres to a squeezer stile before turning left along the narrow path hedged on the right and walled on the left, Beyond the next squeezer stile stay to the right of a barn and cross several fields using a series of obvious stiles until emerging onto the Carperby road. Cross directly to enter the churchyard. By the corner of St Andrew's Church make a left turn to follow your outward route to the Mill Race Tea Shop and, after a relaxing rest, to the car park.

Walk 11: Bolton Castle

Based on an almost impregnable medieval fortress, this route traverses some of the highest ground of central Wensleydale to offer exhilarating views before returning by way of field paths.

Route: Bolton Castle – Ellerlands Edge – Beldon Beck – Low Gate – Ponderledge Scar – Carperby – West Bolton – Bolton Castle.

Start: Car park, Bolton Castle, Wensleydale. Map reference 033019.

Distance: 6 miles (9km)

Map: "The Yorkshire Dales: Northern and Central Areas", number 30 in the O.S. "Outdoor Leisure" series.

Public Transport: Service 157. Leyburn – Hawes. Daily all year except Sundays. Postbus: Northallerton – Bedale – Leyburn – Hawes. All year. Daily except Sundays.

By Car: Bolton Castle is the castle: Castle Bolton the adjacent village. Both are well signed and may be reached by leaving the A684 in Aysgarth and driving through Carperby or Redmire. From Leyburn follow the signed minor roads to Redmire and Bolton Castle. Alternatively, it may be approached from Swaledale by leaving the B6270 at Grinton Bridge and following the signs to Redmire and Bolton Castle.

The Tea Shop

In the days long before tea and coffee had been introduced to English palates several prominent men in history, including Archbishop Scrope of York, had emerged from the Tea Shop at Bolton Castle for their final view of Wensleydale before heading south to London for an appointment with the executioner's block. Appropriately, the present Tea Shop is housed in the former Guest Hall of the Castle where Henry, Lord Percy, (better known as Hotspur in Shakespeare's plays), hatched his unsuccessful plot to oust Henry IV.

Today the only things hatched there are the delicious, mouth-watering concoctions served up to the visiting walker or tourist. The Guest Hall remains very much as it was all those centuries ago. The arched doorways and cavernous stone fireplace are still an integral part of the room and the stone walls, several feet thick, are decorated with tapestries, halberds, pikes and antlers. There are suits of chain mail and one enormous cannon.

There is nothing remotely historical about the food: it is baked freshly on the premises. Sandwiches, with various fillings, are made to order. There is Soup of the Day to be followed by Scones, dripping with cream and jam, Mint Shortbread, Fruit Cake served, as is customary in these parts, with a more than generous wedge of Wensleydale Cheese, Shortbreads, Chocolate Cake, Lemon Cake, Orange Cake and Fat Rascals, all accompanied by a pot of tea or coffee. Opening times: March to November inclusive, daily, 10.00am to 5.00pm. Winter: please ring. Phone 01969 623981.

Bolton Castle

Built in 1379 for Richard le Scrope, Lord Chancellor of England to Richard II, the massive fortress dominates the central areas of Wensleydale. Unlike many such castles, it was also originally designed as a home as well as a fortification, and incorporated most of the then up-to-date facilities. Most of the private living quarters enjoyed their

Bolton Castle

own toilets with plumbing that continued in regular use until the latter part of the nineteenth century.

Bolton Castle suffered little until the Civil war when, serving as a Royalist bastion, it was besieged by Parliamentary forces and suffered an extensive bombardment. As a consequence parts of the north-east tower collapsed a century later. Otherwise the castle remains, very much as it was in the fourteenth century. One distinguished visitor was Mary Queen of Scots when she was being held as a prisoner of Queen Elizabeth I.

Surprisingly for such an important historical building, Bolton Castle is not in public ownership of any kind, either National Trust or English Heritage. It is owned by Mr Harry Orde-Powlett, a direct descendant of the first Lord Scrope. He is continuing with the conservation work initiated by his father in association with English Heritage. In addition to preserving the fabric, he has restored two of the castle's medieval gardens to their former glory. This walk allows time to tour the castle and explore the adjacent village of Castle Bolton. Opening times: March to November: 10.00am to 5.00pm. Winter: please telephone. Phone 01969 623981.

The Route

Turning your back to the castle, take the gravel track which runs alongside the car park in a westerly direction and which is signed to Askrigg. Negotiate the wooden stile by a wooden five-barred gate and, after a further 100 metres, pass through a metal five-barred gate for a fine perspective of Pen Hill, Bishopdale and Waldendale away to your left. Ahead is a fine panorama of Upper Wensleydale with the distinctive shape of Addelborough easy to distinguish.

After passing through another waymarked metal five-barred gate, curve right to another before embarking on a gradual climb onto Ellerlands Edge. Where the track bends towards the left, the going levels to pursue its course over a vast upland pasture where in Spring, skylarks sing, curlews call and lapwings engage in their magical aerial displays.

Pass to the right of a stone barn and then to the left of some wooden farm buildings before starting on a gentle climb for some 350 metres. Stay with the wide track as it turns left through another five-barred gate and then bends to the right, so maintaining the original direction. Initially walk to the left of a wall to cross a beck and pass a waymarked boulder to another gate.

Beyond this the track terminates but a series of waymarked rocks

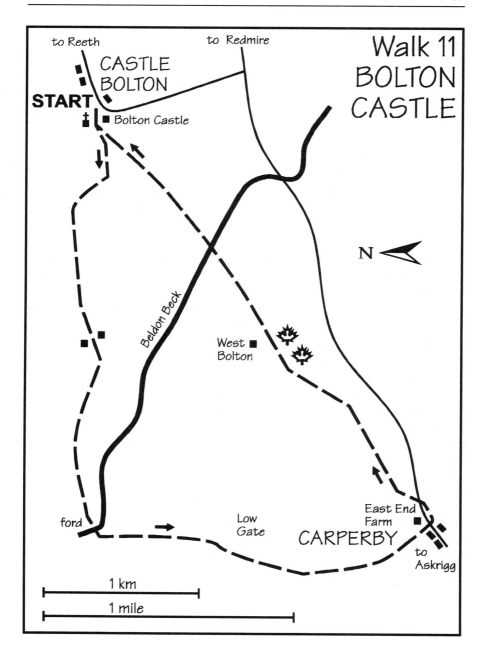

indicate the line of the route as it stays to the right of West Gill. Eventually it crosses the infant Beldon Beck and curves left to a small wooden gate with a finger post alongside.

Through this bear left on a grassy swathe of a path, initially staying to the left of a spasmodic line of trees and then descending from Ellerlands Edge across an enormous pasture while gradually bearing right. On reaching a facing stone wall, turn right and, keeping it on your left, continue to the south-west corner of the field to a three-armed footpath post by a five-barred gate.

Bear left in the direction of Carperby, walking to the right of a wall until the path develops into a wide, stony track. The descent is steep. At the next junction, ignore the track signed to Askrigg. Instead continue forwards and downwards until arriving at a T-junction on the outskirts of the village of Carperby. Turn left to meet the main road.

Turn left again but, after 200 metres and just beyond East End Farm, turn left by a footpath sign. Stay to the left of the wall until meeting a rough track. Turn right through a wooden five-barred gate to climb the track which is signed to Bolton Castle.

After negotiating a waymarked through stile, proceed on a grassy path to the left of a field barn to a waymarked gated stile. Bear right towards the field boundary. Remain along the boundary and to the right of a pond to yet another gated stile. From there take a line on the post by the end of a derelict wall and continue to another stile and footpath finger post.

Proceed to the left of West Bolton Plantation. From the next stile aim for a gated stile and footpath sign some 10 metres to the left of a five-barred gate. Bear left along the track through the yard of West Bolton Farm where, if you are fortunate, you may seem some peacocks and pea hens.

Keeping the house on your left, reach a gated stile and then bear slightly left, staying alongside a wire fence to yet another gated stile. From this point veer right towards a concrete footbridge and proceed up the slope to another stile, this time by a pylon. From there maintain direction guided by Bolton Castle and a series of footpath signs and waymarks to the south-west corner of a small plantation where there is another footpath post. By this make a right turn for about 7 metres and, beyond a gated stile, proceed through the plantation to another stile and the car park.

Walk 12: Jervaulx Abbey

A gentle stroll through the quiet parkland of this Yorkshire abbey where Wensleydale Cheese originated.

Route: Abbey entrance – Abbey ruins – Wind Hills – Kilgram Lane – Jervaulx Park – Abbey entrance.

Start: Car park, Jervaulx Abbey. Map reference 168857.

Distance: 2½ miles (4km)

Map: "Middleham and Jervaulx Abbey", number 630 in the O.S. "Path-finder" series.

Public Transport: Dalesbus service 803: Leeds – Harrogate – Ripon – Reeth – Hawes. Summer Sundays and Bank Holidays only. Harrogate and District Bus Co.
Service X 97: Leeds – Harrogate – Ripon – Richmond. Summer Sundays and Bank Holidays only. Fridays during August. Harrogate and District Bus Co.
Service 160: Leyburn – Thornton Steward. Fridays only. All year. United Bus Co.
Service X 59: Leyburn – Masham – Ripon. Tuesdays, Thursdays and Saturdays only. All year. United Bus Co.

By Car: Jervaulx Abbey is located on the A6108 road between Masham and Middleham. It is well signed and there is a large car park opposite to the Abbey entrance. There is an honesty box for those not visiting the Abbey ruins.

The Tea Shop

There is a light, airy atmosphere to be found in the Tea Room and Visitor centre which stands by the car park at Jervaulx Abbey. It has been created by converting a former bothy and greenhouse. The flagged floors and exposed stone walls, partially decorated by works of a local artist, help to create an unusual, pleasant ambience.

All the dishes and gateaux are freshly cooked on the premises. Lunches are served from midday until 2 p.m. and include such savoury dishes as Yorkshire Rarebit, Welsh Rarebit, Cottage Pie, home-made

Beefburger, Neptune's Seafood and Broccoli Bake. There is a wide selection of sandwiches, both plain and toasted, while Jacket Potatoes with a choice of fillings are also available.

For later in the day there is Afternoon Tea, Cream Tea, Rich Fruit Cake served with Wensleydale Cheese, Hot Buttered Plum Bread, Hot Teacakes made with real tea, Poppy Seed Cake, Lemon Cake, Raspberry Truffle Cake and Chocolate Cake, but to mention a few. All of these may be accompanied by a pot of one of the speciality teas or coffees. Opening times: March to October: daily, 10.00am to 5.00pm. November and December: daily, 12 noon to 4.00pm. Closed Mondays. January and February: closed. Phone 01677 460391.

Jervaulx Abbey

Jervaulx, founded in 1156 close to the banks of the River Ure, was originally a daughter house of Byland Abbey, also in Yorkshire. Traditionally the first Abbot, John of Kinstan, was travelling from Byland to the Abbey of Fors in Scotland when he and his companions became lost in a thick forest. They were guided to safety by a vision of the Virgin Mary who told them, "Ye are late of Byland but now of Yorevale".

Jervaulx Abbey

Yore was the original name of the River Ure. Yorevale was subsequently Gallicised into Jervaulx by a Marchioness of Aylesbury at a
period when French names were fashionable. She was also responsible
for transforming Ryedale into Rievaulx.

Jervaulx was a Cistercian establishment where strict rules applied.
The monks, originally, were not allowed to eat meat, eggs or cheese and
were dedicated to a life of prayer and hard work, mainly farming.

As the Order was of French origin they introduced the art of cheese
making into the area, producing the first Wensleydale and Coverdale
Cheeses. These were of the blue variety, similar to their native Roque-
fort.

As with nearby Fountains Abbey, the community flourished, becom-
ing one of the largest landowners in the Dales, especially in Wensleydale. Their influence spread far and wide and many of the green lanes
used in this collection of walks were established by the monks of
Jervaulx travelling on foot or horseback to supervise their large flocks
of sheep on distant granges.

Unfortunately Adam Sedber, the Abbot at the time of the Reformation, offended Henry VIII who ordered the complete destruction of the
monastic buildings at Jervaulx. Even so, sufficient portions remain to
provide us with some notion of how it must have appeared in its heyday.

These are now in the custody of the Burdon family, thus making them
the only Cistercian ruins in England still in private ownership. At the
time of writing a conservation project is under way to preserve what
still remains standing. Of special interest are the 200 species of wild
flowers which grow amongst and on the ruins. Opening times: As for
the Tea Shop.

The Route

From the car park cross the A6108 to the abbey entrance (honesty box
£0.50 for admission). Cross the wide track and then maintain direction
along the narrower path to visit the ruins.

Afterwards, retrace your steps to the wide gravel track and turn left,
soon passing Abbey Hill on your right. At a junction ignore another
track to the left, along which there is no right of way, and stay forward
to the right of a line of trees. Beyond these the track winds its way
through Wind Hills which, compared with the summits of Upper
Wensleydale, are little more than mounds.

At the next Y-junction fork left, pass to the right of a lake and cross
a cattle grid to meet Kilgram Lane by a lodge and footpath sign. Turn

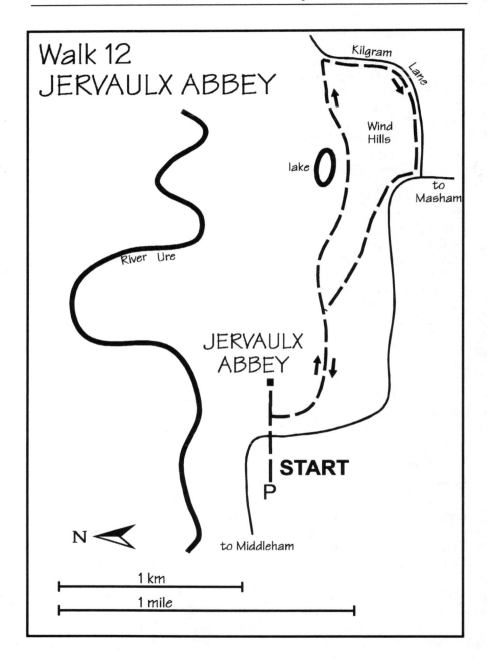

Walk 12
JERVAULX ABBEY

Kilgram Lane

Wind Hills

lake

to Masham

River Ure

JERVAULX ABBEY

START

P

to Middleham

N

1 km

1 mile

right along the surfaced lane which, with its flower-lined verges, passes through a gently undulating landscape until meeting the A6108. At this junction, and by a lodge, turn right through a metal five-barred gate onto another wide track.

Where this curves round to the right, fork left onto an unsigned but clear path which ascends the slight slope to a large wooden and table-like structure. From this summit it loses height while staying to the right of a somewhat substantial stone house to meet the original wide track. Turn left along your outward route.

Walk 13: Middleham

Using field paths and lanes, this route explores a medieval castle before descending into the valley of the River Cover.

Route: Middleham – Castle – William's Hill – Cover Banks – Straight Lane – Chapel Fields – Middleham.

Start: The Square, Middleham. Map reference 127878.

Distance: 3 miles (4.4km)

Map: "The Yorkshire Dales: Northern and Central Areas", number 30 in the O.S. "Outdoor Leisure" series.

Public Transport: Bus service 160: Leyburn – Thornton Steward. Fridays only. United Bus Co.
Bus service 158: Leyburn – Woodale. Fridays only. United Bus Co.
Bus services X 59 and 159: Leyburn – Jervaulx Abbey – Ripon. Tuesdays, Thursdays, Fridays and Saturdays. United Bus Co.
Dalesbus 803: Leeds – Harrogate – Ripon – Leyburn. Summer Sundays and Bank Holidays only. Harrogate and District Bus Co.
Service X 97: Leeds – Harrogate – Ripon – Richmond. Summer Sundays and Bank Holidays only. Also Fridays in August. Harrogate and District Bus Co.

By Car: Middleham lies on the A6108 road between Richmond and Ripon. It may also be approached from Kettlewell by the minor road through Coverdale. There is limited parking in the Square or by the Castle.

The Tea Shop

Located in the Market Square by the corner of Castle Hill, the Castle Keep Tea Room occupies a seventeenth-century listed building. Outside is a notice which reads, "Walkers welcome: muddy boots no problem." That is typical of the hospitality in this corner of Yorkshire. The Castle Keep is run with great enthusiasm and no little panache by Joanne Long who is responsible for all the preserves, marmalades and chutneys bearing the Portcullis label which are for sale.

There is a green and cream colour scheme, an old-fashioned stone fireplace and a display of copper ladles. The crafts on display include horses and knights in armour – both appropriate for this particular North Yorkshire village.

Apart from such standard favourites as Yorkshire, Assam, Earl Grey and Darjeeling, the list of teas reads like a litany of herbs – Camomile, Camomile and Spearmint, Lemon, Jasmine, Fennel and Lemon Balm, Elderflower, Strawberry and Rose, Lemon and Ginger and Mixed Fruits. There is an equally impressive list of coffees while other beverages include quite a few novelties. One which catches the eye is 'King Richard's Desire', an intriguing mixture of Hot Chocolate laced with Whisky and Cream. Partnering this is "Medieval Delight", Hot Chocolate blended with Brandy. Hot Chocolate with Tia Maria and Cream is known as "Plantagenet Tipple".

The "Hearty Yorkshire Sandwich" range includes Coverdale Cheese with Apple and Walnuts, Yorkshire Roast Ham with Peaches and Roast Beef with Banana, Date and walnut. Similar fillings are to be found in the toasted sandwiches while the list of savouries embraces Hot Bacon Roll with Chutney, Home-made Soup, Mushrooms à la Greque and Castle Keep Salad.

Joanne's real speciality, and one of which she is really proud, is her Hot and Sticky Brandy Pudding served with Nutmeg and Cream, although her Squidgy Chocolate Roulade filled with White Chocolate Sauce is a popular favourite with her regular customers.

Her Apple Pie is served with Cream and Coverdale Cheese while her Raspberry and Cinnamon Torte comes to the table complete with Red Berry Coulis and Cream. Her Scones, accompanied by the usual helpings of Cream and Jam, melt in the mouth. Other delicacies include Sticky Ginger Cake with Lemon Butter, Date and Walnut Cake, Chocolate Caramel Shortcake and Mum's Traditional Home Made Fruit Cake with Wensleydale Cheese.

With all these goodies available, it is surprising that anybody even walks as far as the Castle. Opening times: Summer: daily 10.00am to 6.00pm. Winter: Thursday to Sunday 10.00am to dusk. Phone 01969 623665.

Middleham

The village of Middleham is dominated by the extensive and imposing ruins of its formidable castle. The first, erected on William's Hill shortly after the Norman Conquest, was replaced by the present structure in 1170. In 1472 it passed into the ownership of the Duke of Gloucester, later to become King Richard III, through his marriage to Anne Neville,

Middleham Castle

daughter of the Earl of Warwick. The future king and wife made Middleham their principal home throughout the later stages of the Wars of the Roses, leaving only when he was crowned king in 1483. Today, still very impressive, it is in the custodianship of English Heritage.

Middleham is also noted for the breeding and training of racehorses with 5 stables in the village itself and six other in the immediate neighbourhood. Several winners of the Grand National and other classic races have been bred and trained on Middleham Common.

Middleham's right to hold a market was granted in the fourteenth century and confirmed in 1479 by Richard III, an event recalled by the Swine Cross which still stands in the Market Place. The Square is surrounded by some fine Georgian houses and hotels, proof indeed, of the village's importance in the stagecoach era.

The Route

From the Market square turn left by the Castle Keep Tea Room to climb cobbled Castle Hill. At the top cross another narrow cobbled road to enter the wide track running alongside the Castle on its eastern side to reach a metal five-barred gate. By this is a sign indicating a path to Black

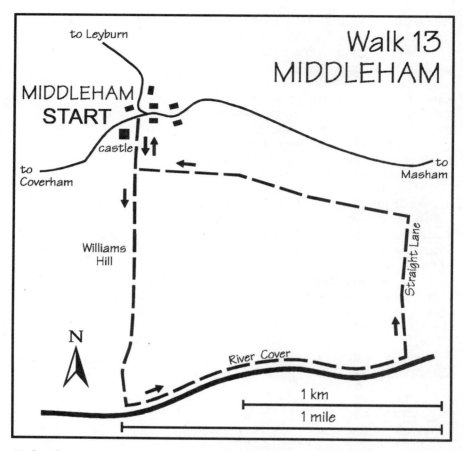

to Leyburn

Walk 13
MIDDLEHAM

MIDDLEHAM
START

castle

to
Masham

to
Coverham

Williams
Hill

Straight Lane

N

River Cover

1 km

1 mile

Dub. Through the gate, follow this path alongside a wall on the right as it climbs towards the crest of the field which offers a fine view into Coverdale, one of the tributaries of the River Ure. Away to the right is William's Hill, the site of Middleham's first castle.

On the crest negotiate a waymarked wooden stile and maintain direction to the right of a wall and a barn. Where the wall terminates, proceed alongside the fence through a shallow valley peppered with stunted hawthorns until reaching the northern banks of the River Cover. On the far side of the river is Cover Scar, a large limestone outcrop

Turn left over a waymarked stile, following the clear path with the river on your right. Pass through a gap in a wall and negotiate a ladder stile which permits entry into a wood where, in Spring, the dominant flora consists of wild garlic, wood anemones and blue bells. The mixture of woodland birdsong is accompanied by the calls of coot, moorhen and mallard from the river.

Still within the wood, the path climbs slightly until it runs above a sharp bend in the river. From there it descends to a wooden kissing gate-cum-stile on the boundary of the wood. Taking your directions from the waymark, bear slightly left across the first meadow to a facing waymarked gateway. Ignore this and the wide track beyond. Instead, remain along the much narrower riverside path to reach a second waymark after a further 100 metres.

Again ignore a rising path to the left, continuing by the River Cover to a set of stepping stones on your right. Do not cross them. Proceed for a further 10 metres to a waymarked stile. Over this, turn left, climbing somewhat steeply to the right of a wall. After 100 metres the gradient eases and the path goes forward to a metal five-barred gate alongside a derelict barn.

This gate provides an entry into Straight Lane. Proceed along the lane until, about 100 metres beyond Chapel Fields Farm which is on your right, turn left through a waymarked squeezer stile. Initially staying to the left of a wall and then using the stiles and waymarks as your guide, cross the pastures until joining your outward route almost by the castle. Turn right for the return into the centre of Middleham and the Castle Keep Tea Room.

Walk 14: Fountains Abbey

A short but fascinating walk which allows time to explore the extensive ruins of this famous Cistercian Abbey, the landscaped gardens, Fountains Hall and the Church of St Mary.

Route:	Visitor Centre – Swanley Grange – Fountains Hall – Fountains Abbey – Anne Boleyn's Seat – Water Gardens – The Lake – Deer Park – St Mary's Church – Visitor Centre.
Start:	Car park by the Visitor Centre. Map reference 271683.
Distance:	2¾ miles (4.4km)
Map:	"Nidderdale", number 26 in the O.S. "Explorer" series.
Public Transport:	Bus service 802: Bradford – Harrogate – Ripon. Sundays only, June to August. Angloblue Bus Co. Bus service 145 from Ripon. Thursdays and Saturdays only. United Bus Co.
By Car:	Fountains Abbey is signed from the B6265 road between Pateley Bridge and Ripon, approximately 4 miles to the west of Ripon. There is a large Pay and Display car park near the Visitor centre.

The Tea Shop

In sharp contrast to the medieval ruins of Fountains Abbey the tea shop, which forms an integral part of the Visitor Centre, is of modern, almost futuristic design. With its ceiling of large, sweeping curves, it is a light, airy building of steel and timber. Mobile screens, with sepia photographs of the Abbey ruins, provide some subdivisions to break-up the vast space.

It is counter service. The wooden tables are accompanied by cane-bottom chairs and there are also tables outside for the more clement weather of summer.

The menu is not for the diet conscious. There is a wide selection of cakes embracing Millionaire's Shortbread, Flapjacks, Yorkshire Ginger Cake, Coffee Cake or Scones with jam and butter or jam and cream. Snacks and light meals are always on offer along with sandwiches, Soup of the Day and a choice between two main courses which vary on a daily basis. Beverages include a variety of teas, coffees and soft drinks. Opening times: April to August: inclusive. Daily. 10.00am to 6.00pm. September to March: 10.00am to 5.00pm or dusk, if earlier. Closed 24th and 25th December and Fridays during January. Phone: 01765 601004.

Fountains Abbey

Deservedly, the ruins of Fountains Abbey, in association with Fountains Hall and the Studley Water Gardens, have long been a magnet for tourists. Despite this, however, the narrow valley of the River Skell, some three miles from Ripon, retains an atmosphere of rural calm and tranquillity. Owned by the National Trust and English Heritage, it has been declared a World Heritage Site.

The Abbey was founded on the 27th December, 1132, by a dissident group of monks from St Mary's Abbey, York. Dissatisfied with the laxer Benedictine Rule, they wished to follow the stricter Cistercian Code then recently introduced by St Bernard of Clairvaux at Citeaux in France. They found a protector in Archbishop Thurstan of York who provided this plot of land by the River Skell. It resembled a miniature

Fountains Abbey

ravine fed by several springs or fountains which soon gave the Abbey its name.

To enable the monks to devote their time more fully to prayer, they introduced a system of lay brothers who also took monastic vows but were housed separately with their own dormitories and refectories. This explains the enormous scale of the buildings at Fountains. Some of these lay brothers worked as masons, carpenters, brewers, smiths and tanners but the majority were involved in supervising the enormous flocks of sheep scattered throughout the Yorkshire Dales on estates owned by the Abbey.

Consequently, Fountains was one of the wealthiest religious foundations in medieval Europe. It passed through several cycles of both spiritual and economic decline and revival until finally closed by Henry VIII's Dissolution of the Monasteries after which the land was sold to Sir Thomas Gresham.

Fountains Hall

The estate was later sold by the Gresham family to Stephen Proctor who was responsible for the construction of Fountains Hall, believed to have been designed by Robert Smythson, the architect of Hardwick Hall in Derbyshire, and built from stone plundered from the Abbey. With its bold outline and Renaissance details, it is typical of the late Tudor period. Over the succeeding centuries it experienced several owners until sold to the Aislabie family in 1768.

The Water Gardens

The originator of the Water gardens was John Aislabie who, as Chancellor of the Exchequer, was implicated in the notorious South Sea Bubble. As a consequence he was barred from holding public office for life. He, therefore, concentrated all his enormous energies on landscaping his estates in Yorkshire, a task continued by his son, William. It was an epic task involving massive engineering works for the construction of lakes and canals and is now regarded as the finest example of a formal garden in Britain, if not in Europe.

Note: there is a charge for admissions to the abbey ruins and water gardens. the visitor centre has a selection of detailed guides to the history of the abbey, Fountains Hall, the water gardens, the deer park and St Mary's church. Phone 01765 608888 for further details of facilities and opening times.

The Route

From the ticket desk in the Visitor Centre continue forwards through the doors into the grounds to reach a Y-junction after a few metres. Fork left, following the wide path signed as "the scenic route", very soon passing through a pair of small wooden gates before turning left. Beyond a second set of gates the path crosses open parkland with Swanley Grange but a short distance away to the right.

On approaching closer to the Abbey Tower and by some iron railings, swing to the right so that the monastic ruins are below on your left. Proceed to meet a junction of paths by Swanley Grange. There, bear left to pass through a metal gate to a T-junction.

Turn right, taking the path signed to Fountains Hall. On reaching the next T-junction, close to the Hall itself, turn right for a view of the noble building. Afterwards retrace your steps to the T-junction and stay forward following a path signed "To The Abbey". Pass through some large wooden gates to another junction complete with footpath finger posts. Stay forward for a closer inspection of the ruins. Otherwise, turn right to cross a small stone bridge encrusted with lichens and carpeted with moss which spans the River Skell.

After 20 metres swing round to the left to enjoy a remarkable view of the Abbey ruins close at hand and then visit the small museum on your right. This houses a display of medieval tiles, a scale model of the Abbey at the height of its glory, a Piscina and a most unusual acoustic jar employed for amplifying the voices of the monks in the choir. Made locally in the late twelfth century, it is an earthenware jar ingeniously set into a block of stone.

Emerging from the museum, continue along the path as it climbs gently to offer a different perspective of the ruins. Ignore an unsigned path branching-off to the left, instead remain with the broader, main path which soon loses altitude to run alongside the River Skell with steeply wooded slopes rising on both sides.

In Spring and early Summer these are bursting with birdsong from the blue tits, great tits, blackbirds, robins, wrens, thrushes, nuthatch and chaffinch while coots, Canada Geese, mute swans and mallard grace the nearby waters.

Continue as far as Half Moon Pond, recognised by its shape. After the second white seat make an acute turn to the right for the steep ascent of the path signed, "High Ride". After approximately 300 metres this curves leftwards while levelling-out to pursue its course along the crest of the ridge and affording occasional glimpses through the trees to the

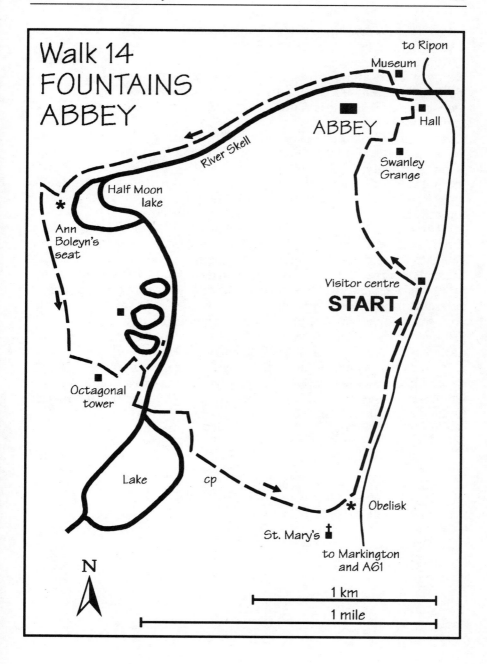

Walk 14
FOUNTAINS
ABBEY

to Ripon

Museum

ABBEY

Hall

Swanley
Grange

River Skell

Half Moon
lake

Ann
Boleyn's
seat

Visitor centre
START

Octagonal
tower

Lake   cp

Obelisk

St. Mary's

to Markington
and A61

N

1 km

1 mile

valley below. From the shelter of Anne Boleyn's Seat there is a breath-taking vista along the valley of the Skell to the Abbey ruins.

Continue along the clear, wide path to the circular Temple of Fame where it bears right to reach a T-junction by the classical Octagon Tower. Turn left, as directed by a sign, to pass through the appropri-ately-named Serpentine Tunnel as it snakes its course through 50 metres of gloom.

After emerging, proceed downhill until meeting a T-junction by the Water Gardens and Moon Pond. Turn left for a few metres to view the Temple of Piety. Otherwise turn right to walk alongside the Canal to the point where it joins the Lake by a set of stone pillars. Turn left to cross the Canal, either by using the stepping stones or the wooden footbridge.

At the far end turn right, pass the Lakeside Tea Room (open daily April to September from 10.00am to 5.30pm) and proceed through the gate into Lakeside car park. Bear left up the slope to the obvious footpath finger post. Cross the junction directly to take the grassy footpath signed to St Mary's Church. This initially climbs a shallow valley before emerging into the Deer Park with its large herd of Fallow Deer. The path crosses the open ground towards the splendid church of St Mary. A product of the religious fervour of the nineteenth century, this was designed by William Burgess and is noted for its fine interior.

In front of the church turn left along the surfaced driveway to reach a set of gates by the Obelisk. Pass through the narrower one and turn left along the signed bridleway which runs for several hundred metres to the car park and Visitor Centre.

Walk 15: Middlesmoor

An exhilarating and strenuous walk which offers fine views of Upper Nidderdale as a reward.

Route: How Stean Gorge – Middlesmoor – Northside Head – How Gill – Limley Farm – Thrope Edge – Lofthouse – How Stean Gorge.

Start: Car park, How Stean Gorge. Map reference 095735.

Distance: 6 miles (9.6km)

Maps: "Nidderdale", number 26 in the O.S. "Explorer" series *or* "The Yorkshire Dales: Northern and Central Areas", number 30 in the O.S. "Outdoor Leisure" series.

Public Transport: None.

By Car: From Pateley Bridge follow the unclassified road signed to Lofthouse and Middlesmoor. Just beyond Lofthouse turn left along the lane signed to How Stean Gorge. There is a car park for café patrons and visitors to the Gorge.

The Tea Shop

In recent years the facilities at the How Stean Gorge café have been vastly improved with respect to the accommodation and the fare on offer. The menu is wide-ranging, catering for everyone from those in need of a substantial repast to the seeker after a simple cup of tea. There is the usual choice of sandwiches from Roast Ham to Wensleydale Cheese and, on Sundays, the traditional Yorkshire Pudding and Roast Beef. The cakes and scones on display are all home-made and served, if desired, with generous helpings of cream. Opening times: Daily, all year, 10.00am to 6.00pm. Closed Mondays and Tuesdays in January and February. Phone 01423 755666.

How Stean Gorge

Often referred to as "Yorkshire's Little Switzerland", How Stean Gorge is a steep-sided limestone ravine some 25 metres deep in places. A series of specially constructed footpaths and bridges allow the visitor to explore the area where water rushes over large boulders. The sides are clothed with mosses, lichens and ferns while oak, ash and hazel provide a green canopy in Summer. There is also an opportunity to explore Tom Taylor's Cave which is entered down a flight of steps from the gorge itself. Opening times: Daily, all year, 10.00am to 6.00pm. There is an admission charge.

Middlesmoor

Standing at over 300 metres (1,000 feet) above sea level, Middlesmoor is a fine example of an upland village. Although small, with its houses huddled closely together, it boasts a church, a pub and a post office. It also offers magnificent views down the length of Nidderdale towards Gouthwaite Reservoir and Pateley Bridge.

An attractive house at Middlesmoor

The Route

Leave the car park entrance by turning right into the lane and following it for several hundred metres to a green caravan on your right. Immediately beyond, and by a Nidderdale Way sign and another to Middlesmoor, turn right through a squeezer stile so that the caravan is on your right with a wall on your left.

Advance 20 metres to a second squeezer stile and a memorial stone set into the wall. This is dedicated to Jennie Jefferson who was born at Stean on the 4th February, 1918.

Proceed to the left of a wire fence, losing height to a footbridge over How Steen Beck before climbing some steps to a small wooden gate and another Nidderdale Way sign. Through the gate bear right, heading diagonally right to a waymarked squeezer stile before turning left to walk just to the right of a wall for 50 metres to another stile. With the village of Middlesmoor in sight, remain to the right of the wall as you climb. Negotiate two further squeezer stiles to emerge onto the road. Turn left and follow this as it rises steeply, twisting and turning to the village centre. Continue between the houses, passing the Wesleyan Chapel, built in 1899 and now a private residence, the pub and the Post Office on your way.

Just beyond the last house, and by 2 telegraph poles and a red box, turn right into a lane.

Almost immediately make a left turn through a squeezer stile onto an unsigned path. Keep straight ahead, clipping a wall corner to another stile and then proceed to the right of a wall to a wooden stile. Remain to the left of a small plantation for 20 metres to a through stile.

Beyond this turn sharply to the right to pass some 30 metres to the left of a field barn before negotiating a gated stile. Continue, with a fence on your right, towards Smithfield Hall. With the Hall on your immediate right, bear left to a waymarked squeezer stile in the facing wall and maintain the line of direction across the middle of the field to another through stile.

Advance along the clear path to a waymarked stile which provides access to a lane. Turn right to pass Northside Farm and, a short distance afterwards, negotiate two waymarked wooden five-barred gates within 75 metres of each other. From this point there are some splendid view towards the moors surrounding the head of Nidderdale.

Stay with this green lane along the contour before losing height slightly to a third five-barred gate. Cross several culverted becks while gradually losing further altitude to yet another metal five-barred gate, this one close to the corner of How Gill Plantation, which is on your left.

Pass through this five-barred gate but, immediately, make a right turn through a second before veering left down the steep slope to the far corner of the field, crossing a stream on the way.

In the field corner turn right, as indicated by a waymark on a tree, to

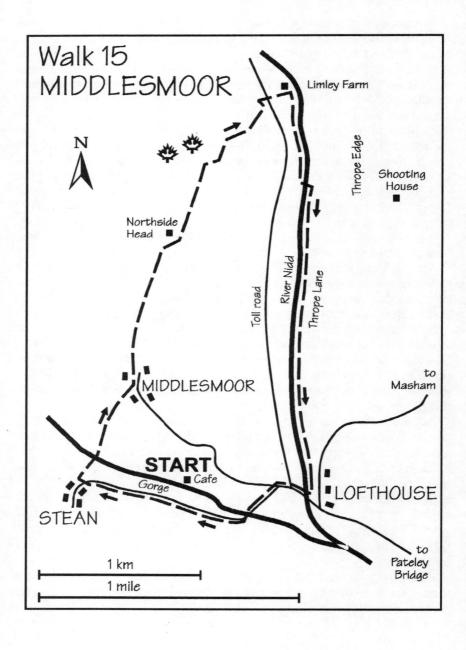

Walk 15
MIDDLESMOOR

N

Limley Farm

Thrope Edge

Shooting
House

Northside
Head

River Nidd

Toll road

Thrope Lane

to
Masham

MIDDLESMOOR

START
Cafe

Gorge

LOFTHOUSE

STEAN

to
Pateley
Bridge

1 km

1 mile

negotiate a through stile. From there take your direction from that waymark and head across the next field while staying to the left of a stream to gain the left-hand corner of a field barn. Pass through the gap between the end of the barn and a drystone wall before turning sharp left to walk close to the wall on your left. Eventually bear slightly right towards an obvious stile in the facing wall, positioned some 50 metres to the right of the field corner. Cross the next field diagonally right to a stone step stile before advancing a further 50 metres to a squeezer stile in a fence and descending a flight of steps to reach the toll road which leads to Scar House Reservoir.

Cross this road directly to a squeezer stile and then advance to the left of an open barn and the outbuildings of Limley Farm and a second squeezer stile in a stone wall. This provides access onto a lane. Turn right to a Nidderdale Way sign after 40 metres.

Continue to a waymarked wooden stile and then turn left for 20 metres to the next Nidderdale Way sign. Turn right alongside a fence but, after a further 30 metres, turn left over a stile and then immediately right to accompany the infant Nidd, nothing more than a trickle at this location. After 200 metres turn right over a waymarked ladder stile and then left to proceed to the right of a fence until reaching a wooden five-barred gate.

Through this, use the large stone slabs to cross to the eastern bank of the river. Make a right turn so that you are now to the left of the Nidd. Where the path meets a wall-cum-fence follow it round towards the left to another five-barred gate beyond which the path widens into Thrope Lane which takes its name from Thrope Edge, high above to your left. This green lane, with its turf surface makes for excellent walking while offering delectable views of both sides of this upland valley. For a short distance it climbs gently but, having passed to the left of Thrope Farm, begins to lose height to a wooden five-barred gate before climbing again. Having lost its walls, it runs through open country with the Nidd some distance below on the right.

The going levels by the boundary wall of a plantation and, having negotiated more five-barred gates, forms a junction with a minor road by a Nidderdale Way sign.

Turn right along the road as it drops steeply into the village of Lofthouse. Pause to examine the War Memorial which also serves as the village fountain. It carries this inscription:

> *"If you want to be healthy, wealthy and stout*
> *Use plenty of cold water inside and out.*
> *Let animal and man drink freely".*

By the War Memorial turn right to pass between the ends of two rows of cottages, one of which is named "Fountain Cottage". By this take the track on the right which bends left across a stone bridge spanning the Nidd to a road.

Cross this directly to a kissing gate and follow a path signed to Middlesmoor. Stay to the right of a fence and to the left of some cattle sheds. Where the fence ends, bear right to a kissing gate which allows access onto the road to Middlesmoor. Turn right for 100 metres and then left into the surfaced lane signed to How Stean Gorge and follow it round to the car park at How Stean Gorge.

Walk 16: Pateley Bridge

A steep climb above the River Nidd provides extensive panoramic vistas of Nidderdale before a return along a pleasant riverside path.

Route: Pateley Bridge – St Mary's Church – Knott – Kiln Hill – Glasshouses – Pateley Bridge.

Start: Southfield car park, Pateley Bridge. Map reference 157655.

Distance: 3 miles (4.8km)

Map: "Nidderdale", number 26 in the O.S. "Explorer" series.

Public Transport: Bus service 24: Harrogate – Pateley Bridge. Frequent buses daily, Mondays to Saturdays. More restricted service on Summer Sundays. No service on Winter Sundays. Harrogate and District Bus Co. Service 802: Bradford – Leeds – Otley – Ripon. Summer Sundays and Bank Holidays only. Angloblue Bus Co.

By Car: Pateley Bridge is on the B6265 road from Threshfield to Ripon. It may also be reached by the B6165 from Harrogate and the B6451 from Otley.

The Tea Shop

To enter the Apothecary's House Tea Rooms in Pateley Bridge is, literally, to take a step back into history. The thick wooden beams, oak panelling and stout stone walls are sufficient testimony to the age of the building. It is the oldest house in Pateley Bridge, a claim substantiated by the date, 1635, carved over the stone fireplace in one of the two rooms. Its next door neighbour is also reputed to be the oldest sweet shop in Britain. The beams are decorated with what must certainly be the largest collection of jugs in Yorkshire.

It is many years since the apothecary dispensed his last medicines but today Wendy Dean and her staff dispense food of the highest order including their famous Yorkshire Puddings and, another speciality of the house, Welsh Rarebit. In addition there is home-made Soup, sandwiches, both toasted and plain, Omelettes and Jacket Potatoes with a wide offering of fillings.

There is a choice between Afternoon Tea and Cream Tea as well as

The Apothecary Tea Rooms

a bewildering array of mouth-watering cakes, all freshly baked on the premises. They include Lemon, Chocolate, Coffee, Walnut and Flapjacks. For that drink there is a choice of both speciality teas and coffees. Opening times: Mondays to Saturday, all year: 10.30am to 5.30pm. (Closed Tuesdays). Sundays, all year, 10.30am to 6.00pm. Phone 01423 711767.

Pateley Bridge

The name of this bustling small town means "Path through the glade". The original settlement, dating from the twelfth century, probably occupied a site close to the church of St Mary but the present south-facing location makes an ideal sun-trap. The town was granted a market charter in 1320 but the weekly Tuesday Market has long since disappeared. The first mention of a bridge was in 1320 although the present structure is believed to have been built in the eighteenth century.

At this time Pateley Bridge was noted mainly for its quarries, the stone being in demand nation-wide. The remains of this industry are still to be observed scattered around the neighbouring fells while the tracks, once used by the quarrymen, form the basis of today's splendid footpath network.

In the town centre is the Nidderdale Museum, housed in the former workhouse and boasting lively displays on the history and social life of the district.

The Route

Exit the Southfield car park by turning right into High Street and climbing by the shops for approximately 300 metres to a junction. Turn right into Ripon Road. Just beyond the Methodist Church, which is on your right and by a sign reading, "Panorama Walk, make a left turn up a flight of stone steps followed by a flagged path. Soon the flags give way to a tarmac surface but the walled lane continues its steep, upwards course until the houses are left behind and a glorious panorama of Nidderdale presents itself.

Pass to the right of the cemetery and, by the gates, fork left up another narrow lane. By the far end of the cemetery turn left up a short flight of steps and follow the path to the ruins of St Mary's Church, site of the original settlement of Pateley Bridge. Afterwards, retrace your steps to the lane and turn left, still climbing.

Before the gradient eventually levels there is a small iron gate on the right. Pass through this to reach a dramatic viewpoint from where Yorke's Folly and Greenhow Hill are clearly visible across the valley. Closer to hand, the slopes below the viewing platform are carpeted with bluebells in Spring.

Continue along the walled lane as it runs along the crest of Ripley Bank, until finally reaching the tiny settlement of Knott. By "Cross Lane House" stay forward for 100 metres to a bend in the road with a footpath sign adjacent. Leave the road and maintain direction along a rough lane. After 50 metres ignore a footpath sign on the left indicating a footpath to Blazefield. Instead maintain your line of direction along the track to pass to the left of a white house and to enjoy unparalleled views out over Summer Bridge.

On reaching a T-junction turn right along another walled lane, losing altitude until meeting the B6265 Pateley Bridge to Ripon road by Kiln Hill Farm.

Turn right and exercise extreme caution because of the bends until reaching a pavement after 100 metres. Continue for a further 120 metres to the junction with the Harrogate road. Turn right for 100 metres. Turn left across the road to a footpath sign. Having negotiated the metal

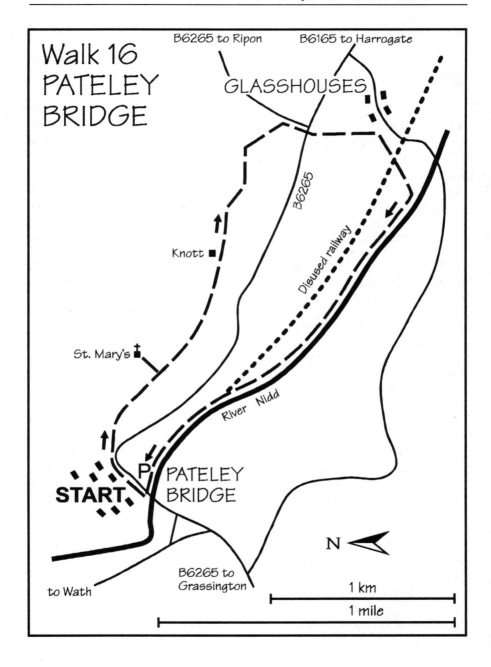

Walk 16
PATELEY
BRIDGE

B6265 to Ripon

B6165 to Harrogate

GLASSHOUSES

B6265

Disused railway

Knott

St. Mary's

River Nidd

START

P PATELEY BRIDGE

to Wath

B6265 to Grassington

N

1 km

1 mile

kissing gate alongside, take the flagged path to the left of a stone house and descend the field with a wall on your right. After another gate continue down the next field but now to the right of a wall. Pass between the houses to emerge onto a lane on the outskirts of the village of Glasshouses.

Turn right along this lane to pass Westfields Farm and descend a slope to a facing five-barred gate. Do not go through this but stay with the lane as it bends to the left and crosses a railway bridge spanning the former Harrogate to Pateley Bridge Railway.

Ignore the stile on the right at the far end of the bridge. Instead, pass through the facing gateway before turning sharply to the right and aiming for a gateway in the facing wall. Through that veer leftwards over the crest of a large field before losing height slightly to an official wall gap and descending three steps onto the riverside path. Turn right along this and, with the Nidd on your left, follow it to the bridge at the end of High Street in Pateley Bridge. Turn right for Southfields car park.

Walk 17: Grimwith

After climbing over high moorland and encircling a reservoir noted
for its wildlife, this route returns to one of the most famous show
caves in the Yorkshire Dales.

Route: Stump Cross Caverns – Nursery Knott – Knott Head – High Shaws
                      Laithe – Grimwith Beck – Bracken Haw – Far Rams Close – Grimwith
                      car park – Rough Hill – Nursery Knott – Stump Cross Caverns.

Start: Stump Cross Caverns. Map reference 089635.

Distance: 7½ miles (12km)

Maps: "Nidderdale", number 26 in the O.S. "Explorer" series *or* "The York-
                      shire Dales: Southern Area", number 10 in the O.S. "Outdoor Lei-
                      sure" series.

Public Transport: Bus service 802: Bradford – Leeds – Ripon. Summer Sundays and
                      Bank Holidays only. Angloblue Bus Co.
                      Bus service 24: Harrogate – Pateley Bridge – Grassington. Summer
                      Sundays and Bank Holidays only. Harrogate and District Bus Co.

By car: Stump Cross Caverns are situated on the B6265 road between
                      Pateley Bridge and Grassington. There is an area of waste ground
                      approximately 200 metres west of Stump Cross Caverns suitable for
                      off-road parking.

The Tea Shop

The Tea Rooms at Stump Cross Caverns are housed within the Visitor
Centre with its displays, souvenirs and rock samples. The windows
command some excellent views over the surrounding moorlands and
across southern Wharfedale. There is a light, airy atmosphere with the
pristine white walls and carpeted floors. The wooden tables are partnered by spindle-backed chairs and there is a large iron stove in the
fireplace.

It is counter service with a range of meals to suit all appetites
including Breaded Scampi, Breaded Haddock, Chicken Kiev and
Caver's Breakfast. In a somewhat lighter vein comes Beans on Toast and
Cheese on Toast while Sticky Toffee Pudding is something of a speci-

ality of the house. The large selection of cakes includes Scones, with or without Cream, Millionaire's Shortbread, Chocolate Cake, Walnut Cake and Lemon Cake, but to name a few. And, to accompany all of these, there is a choice of tea, coffee or soft drinks. Opening times: Mid-March to Mid-November: daily 10.00am to 6.00pm. Winter: Saturdays and Sundays, 10.00am to dusk. Phone: 01756 752780.

Stump Cross Caverns

Stump Cross Caverns are one of the major show caves of Yorkshire. Discovered during the nineteenth century when lead miners were sinking a shaft near Stump Cross. They came across the caves at a depth of 15 metres and subsequent exploration revealed a labyrinth of subterranean passages rich with stalagmite and stalactite formations. The caves have yielded a rich harvest of animal bones and remains believed to be between 30,000 and 200,000 years old. These include bison, reindeer, fox, wolf and wolverine. Today the caverns have been professionally illuminated and may be visited using special gravel paths.

Grimwith Reservoir

The original reservoir was constructed in 1884 to supply the water needs of Otley and Bradford. It was vastly extended in 1987, the old embankment being incorporated within the new. As a result Grimwith has become the largest expanse of water in Yorkshire. It holds 21,770,000 cubic metres of water.

In recent years Yorkshire Water PLC has created permissive footpaths to enable a complete circuit of the reservoir to be walked. Sailing is permitted although large areas are out of bounds because they have been specially reserved for wildlife. Trees have been planted in co-operation with the Yorkshire Dales National Park and the RSPB. Amongst the species of bird that breed on or around the reservoir thanks to this enlightened policy, are short-eared owl, widgeon. common sandpiper, teal, oystercatcher, curlew, little ringed plover, Canada Geese, lapwing and both pied and yellow wagtail. Some of the stone walls around Grimwith provide shelter and habitat for stoats which are a common sight.

On this walk you will pass High Laithe Barn, a listed building and one of the most unusual barns in Yorkshire. Its raised cruck frame has been thatched with ling or heather as distinct from being roofed with

Thatched Cruck Barn

stone. Since the reservoir was extended, Yorkshire Water PLC has been responsible for not only conserving but restoring this unique building.

The Route

From Stump Cross Caverns turn left along the B6265 and walk in a westerly direction for approximately 200 metres. At the bottom of the hill, turn right across a piece of waste ground (suitable for parking) to negotiate a stile alongside a five-barred gate and a footpath sign indicating a route to Grimwith Reservoir.

Climb to the left of a drystone wall and, where this corners away to the right, maintain your direction up the slope guided by a line of yellow-topped waymarker posts. As you get higher there is an ever-expanding panorama of Lower Wharfedale behind, with the Barden Fells and Simon's Seat prominent on a clear day. Closer to hand, in Spring and early Summer, lapwing wheel and plummet while skylarks provide a constant source of music.

At the summit pass to the right of Nursery Knott and then bear left behind it to a ladder stile with a footpath post adjacent. Immediately over this first stile, turn through ninety degrees to the right and climb

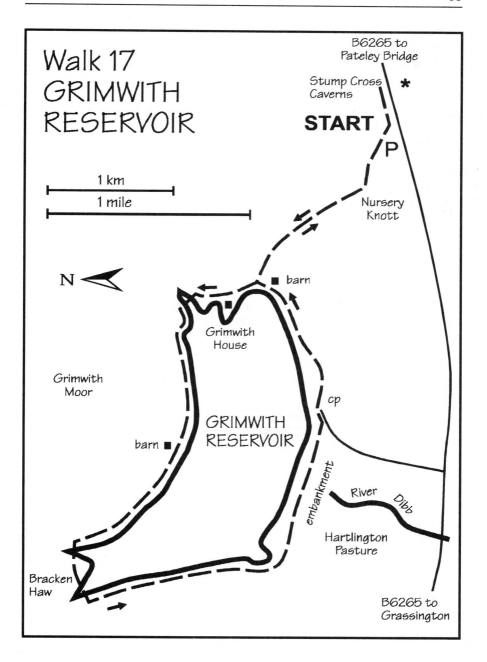

Walk 17
GRIMWITH
RESERVOIR

B6265 to
Pateley Bridge

Stump Cross
Caverns

START

P

Nursery
Knott

1 km

1 mile

N

barn

Grimwith
House

Grimwith
Moor

cp

barn

GRIMWITH
RESERVOIR

embankment

River   Dibb

Hartlington
Pasture

Bracken
Haw

B6265 to
Grassington

a second ladder stile before veering leftwards to follow another series of waymarker posts as the going levels.

By the second of these gradually bear towards the right, pass through a derelict wall and then stay approximately 30 metres to the right of another wall, losing altitude to a footpath post.

By this turn left over a stone step stile and continue along the clearly defined and waymarked path as it traverses a stretch of boggy terrain with Grimwith Reservoir easing into sight ahead. Beyond a wooden stile, also accompanied by a footpath sign, bear right over a planked footbridge and advance for 50 metres to a second sign. By this turn right over a ladder stile and bear left to pass to the left of a stone barn on your way to a gated stile. Proceed along the same bearing over the following field to a three-armed footpath post and a stile which allows access to the wide gravel track surrounding Grimwith Reservoir.

Turn right to pass Grimwith House, now deserted, and, just beyond Cadger Beck.

Negotiate a wooden five-barred gate and cross Middle Tongue with a new plantation on your left. Cross Grimwith Beck which flows into the reservoir from Trunla Gill. Stay with this main track as it crosses Sandy Sike and skirts the base of Limekiln Ridge, Grimwith Moor and Appletreewick Moor.

Having passed a ruined farmhouse on your left and a barn on your right stay forward, as directed by a footpath sign, along a somewhat narrower path to a wooden kissing gate. After several hundred metres this path curves round to the right and climbs slightly above the reservoir. It crosses a wooden footbridge spanning Hollin Kell Dike before eventually levelling to accompany a fence on your right.

The narrow, stony path shortly loses altitude to a kissing gate after which it reverts to a wide track at water level before turning right into the mouth of Gate Up Gill with its rocky escarpments such as Tage Bale, Red Scar and Black Crag Moss. This tranquil and seemingly remote spot, cradled by sweeping moorlands, makes an ideal spot for a coffee break and a spot of contemplation.

Soon the track goes through a U-turn over a substantial wooden bridge to climb Bracken Haw. It levels and soon descends to another stout wooden bridge over Blea Gill where another pause is called for to admire the grandeur of Grime Lodge Crags.

Stay with the track as it bends to the left for a gradual climb beneath Hebden Moor until eventually reaching a three-armed finger post at Far Rams Close.

Ignore the bridleway sign indicating Hartlington Moor Lane as a link to the Grassington road. Instead, turn left along the permissive footpath signed "To the Embankment". Initially walk between a wall on the right and a fence on the left, losing height slightly. After 100 metres, and by a stone barn, turn right through a gateway and follow the wonderful grassy path to a stile. Over that swing right, walking between walls for a further 300 metres to a stile adjacent to a wooden five-barred gate. Turn left over this to cross the gentle turf of the embankment of the reservoir.

To the right there is an excellent aerial perspective of the River Dibb flowing down the narrow valley towards Dibbles Bridge. At the nether end of the embankment pass through a small gate and turn left up the slope to reach a footpath finger post by the entrance to the car park.

Turn left, keep the car park on your right and continue along the gravel track to a gated step stile alongside a five-barred gate. After a further 100 metres, and by another footpath sign, fork left along a narrow path which loses height to water level, crossing a wooden footbridge on the way. By the thatched cruck barn it re-joins the wider track. Turn left along this but, after a short distance and by the next footpath finger post, turn right over a stile to retrace your steps by Nursery Knott to Stump Cross Caverns and that well deserved cup of tea.

Walk 18: Ilkley

A steep climb onto Yorkshire's most famous moor is followed by a traverse along the contour which provides panoramic views over Lower Wharfedale.

Route: The Grove – Wells Road – White Wells – West Rock – Ilkley Crags – Backstone Beck – Cow and Calf – The Tarn – The Grove.

Start: Car park, Grove Arcade, Ilkley. Map reference 115476.

Distance: 3½ miles (6.2km)

Map: "Lower Wharfedale & Washburn Valley", number 27 in the O.S. "Explorer" series.

Public Transport: Ilkley is served by frequent trains daily, including Sundays, from Leeds, Bradford and Shipley. There are frequent daily buses, including Sundays, from Leeds, Bradford, Skipton, Harrogate, Knaresborough and York.

By Car: Ilkley is located on the A65 between Skipton and Leeds. There are several car parks in the town centre (Pay and Display).

The Tea Shop

Betty's Tea Rooms stand in the Grove, Ilkley. The glass and cast-iron balustrade over the entrance signals the restrained elegance to be encountered inside. The white and cream ceiling and walls, partially stained-glass windows, inlaid marble tables with cane-bottomed chairs and the potted palms are reminders of an era long since departed. The waitresses, with their white blouses and black skirts provide a smiling, friendly service which more establishments should emulate.

Frederick Belmont, a Swiss confectioner, visited the Yorkshire Dales early this century and was so impressed by the clean air that he decided to settle, opening his first Betty's Tea Room in Harrogate in 1919. During the following decades he established others in York, Ilkley and Northallerton. These are still owned and managed by his descendants.

One of the secrets of Betty's success is that all four hundred items on the menu – bread, cakes, scones, savouries, chocolates and muffins – are still made by hand on the premises. They even select, import and blend their own teas which include China Gui Hua, Zulu, Blue Sapphire and Flowery Orange Pekoe. These are matched by a range of coffees which embraces Coral Island, Monsoon Malabar Mysore, Hawaiian Kona Kai and Celebes Kalossi, not to mention the more popular names of Jamaica Blue Mountain, Peaberry and Puerto Rico Yauco.

The menu is a blend of the two finest cuisines in the world – Yorkshire and Swiss. A day tramping over Ilkley Moor should provide an appetite for Betty's Welsh Rarebit which is cooked with Theakston's Ale and served with Tomato Chutney or a Swiss Alpine Macaroni consisting of Bacon and sliced New Potatoes in a fresh cream sauce and topped with Raclette Cheese. For something a little lighter there is a Yorkshire Fat Rascal, a plump fruity scone with citrus peels, spices, almonds and cherries covered with butter, or perhaps a large slice of Yorkshire Curd Tart.

Betty's offers a choice of more than 75 varieties of cakes and pastries including Apple Strudel, Normandy Pear Torte, Fruit and Cream Heart, Chocolate Mousse Torte or Chocolate Brandy Roulade but to mention a few. Cream Teas and Afternoons Teas are also available. With such a range of choice and quality, allied with exemplary service, Betty's is a real mecca after a day on the hills. And, if you have enjoyed your treat or fancy a different one, you may make a purchase in the shop.

It is advisable to remove your muddy boots before entering. Opening times: Daily, all year, (including Sundays) 9.00am to 6.00pm. Phone 01943 608029.

Ilkley

"On Ilkla Moor baht 'at" has become Yorkshire's National Anthem and provided this moorland spa town with an international reputation. According to local tradition the song was composed by a Halifax church choir as they sat enjoying a picnic by the Cow and Calf Rocks.

Ilkley has enjoyed a long history. There is ample evidence on the moors of prehistoric man in the Cup-And-Ring marked rocks and the mysterious Swastika Stone beyond Hebers Ghyll. The Romans constructed a fort on the site now occupied by the medieval Manor House while the parish church houses a collection of Saxon crosses.

Although little more than a moorland village until the nineteenth century, Ilkley could boast a church before the Norman Conquest and its Grammar School dates from 1637. The famous Old Bridge spanning the River Wharfe and now the starting point for the Dales Way, a long distance footpath, was erected in 1673.

White Wells, Ilkley Moor

Ilkley, however, came to prominence in the middle of the eighteenth century when Squire Middleton opened two open-air spa baths at White Wells. These were filled by a mineral spring at the rate of 100 gallons a minute. This led to the development of the town as a fashionable spa and by the close of the nineteenth century there were 15 hydros.

The arrival of the railway brought the wealthy woollen merchants of Leeds and Bradford who built large houses and, in so doing, initiated the growth of Ilkley as a fashionable shopping centre. With the decline of the spa, Ilkley developed as a holiday venue and tourist centre on the edge of the Yorkshire Dales.

The Route

From the car park exit onto The Grove and make a left turn before proceeding a few metres to the road junction by the Midland Bank. Turn right into Wells Road for the steep climb, continuing beyond Queen's Road and Skelda Rise to Crossbeck Road which is on your left.

There, stay forward through a wooden gate to cross a cattle-grid, but immediately fork left along a clear path which continues climbing to a small pond or mere. Turn left and, by the far corner of the pond, make a right turn up a flight of steps to pass a wooden shelter on your left.

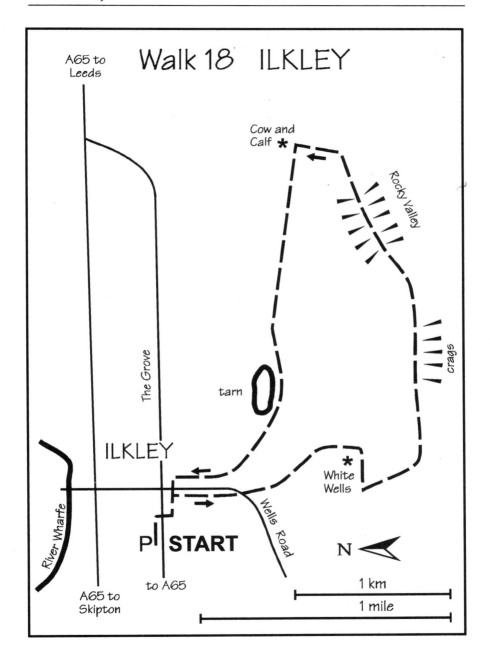

Walk 18 ILKLEY

A65 to Leeds

Cow and Calf *

Rocky Valley

The Grove

tarn

crags

ILKLEY

White Wells *

River Wharfe

Wells Road

P START

to A65

A65 to Skipton

N

1 km

1 mile

Ahead are the bracken and heather covered slopes of Ilkley Moor with the building at White Wells very prominent some distance above. Remain with the clear, distinct path, stepped in sections, until arriving at White Wells. After pausing to admire the view, pass to the left of the white building and then corner it to walk between it and the Spring with its stone canopy which stands on your left.

Some 20 metres beyond the next corner of the Bath House veer left up a broad, stony track. After a further steep climb the gradient eases, the track bends round to the left and runs along the foot of Ilkley Crags. At a Y-junction at the foot of a long flight of steps, fork left along a narrower, sandy path which stays with the contour and creates ideal walking conditions while providing a vista out over the town below and to the moors beyond, including Beamsley Beacon.

After a considerable distance the path climbs once more before levelling to pass through Rocky valley, a sombre defile littered with large boulders shattered from the crag face by frost and rain. The path climbs out of this valley to reach an intersection in the path network from where there is another superb view.

At the intersection fork slightly leftwards and lose some height to pass a small waterfall in Backstone Beck. Stay forward across the stream and, at the far side, turn left for approximately 20 metres to a second intersection. Make a right turn and pass a very large boulder on your right before arriving shortly at a T-junction. Turn right across a level plateau where the springy, turf path provides some relief to the feet. Stay to the right of a large, abandoned quarry to arrive at the celebrated Cow and Calf Rocks, long the haunt of climbers.

From the Cow and Cow Rocks turn round and, immediately, fork right, so keeping the abandoned quarry on your left. Follow the clear, green path as it begins to lose altitude in rounding the quarry and passing through a belt of coniferous trees.

At the first junction, by a large entrance into the quarry, fork right down the slope to another T-junction. Turn left and continue to lose altitude. The path eventually levels and runs parallel to the road below on your right. Descend a flight of steps, cross the wooden footbridge spanning Backstone Beck and remain with the path to The Tarn.

Walk to the left of the water and then proceed along the wide track. After several hundred metres, negotiate a wooden five-barred gate and turn right into Wells Road for the final steep descent into the town centre. At the junction by the traffic lights turn left into The Grove for that well-deserved treat at Betty's.

Walk 19: Bolton Abbey

An exploration of Lower Wharfedale using tracks and field and riverside paths.

Route: Bolton Abbey – Waterfall Bridge – Storiths – Beamsley Hospital – Beamsley Village – Bolton Bridge – Bolton Abbey.

Start: Car park, Bolton Abbey. Map reference 072538.

Distance: 3½ miles (6.2km)

Maps: "The Yorkshire Dales: Southern Area", number 10 in the O.S. "Outdoor Leisure" series *or* "Lower Wharfedale & Washburn Valley", number 27 in the O.S. "Explorer" series.

Public Transport: Dalesbus service 800: Leeds – Bradford – Ilkley – Hawes. Summer Saturdays, Sundays and Bank Holidays. Also Tuesdays in late July and August. Keighley and District Bus Co.
Dalesbus service 800: Harrogate – Hawes. Summer Sundays and Bank Holidays only. Harrogate and District Bus Co.
Dalesbus service 899: Skipton/Ilkley – Grassington – Buckden. Summer Sundays and Bank Holidays only. Pride of the Dales Bus Co.

By Car: Bolton Abbey is signed from the A59 at Bolton Bridge. It is one mile north of Bolton Bridge on the B6160 Bolton Bridge to Aysgarth road. There is a large car park in the village opposite the entrance to the Abbey grounds. Fee payable but the ticket is valid on the same day for other car parks operated by the Bolton Abbey Estate.

The Tea Shop

The Bolton Abbey Tea Cottage is housed in a former tithe barn of uncertain date, although it is thought unlikely to have co-existed with the Priory. It was first shown on a map of 1780 but, a century later, had been converted into two cottages occupied by estate workers and their families.

The cottages became redundant in 1977 and, within two years, had been adapted for their present purpose with several rooms, both upstairs and downstairs, forming the actual Tea Rooms. In view of their pedigree it is hardly surprising that they have oak pillars and beams with thick stone walls. The plain wooden tables and chairs blend perfectly with their ambience as do the floral curtains.

Bessie Barker offers an extremely tempting array of home-made cakes and gateaux including Lemon Meringue Pie, Chocolate and Raspberry Roulade, Carrot Cake, Fruit Pies with Cream, Sticky Toffee Pudding and Lemon Curd Cake, all served with a choice of speciality teas and coffees or soft drinks.

There is a choice of Afternoon Tea or Cream Tea while the blackboard lists the Daily Specials ranging from Deep-Fried Mushrooms or Chicken Provençal to Welsh Rarebit or Haddock Au Gratin, not to mention Cumberland Sausage, Quiche Lorraine and Omelettes. Opening times: Easter to late October: daily, 9.30am to 6.00pm. Winter: Saturdays and Sundays only, 9.30am to 6.00pm. Phone 01756 710495.

Bolton Abbey

The name Bolton Abbey has long been applied to both the historical; ruins and the nearby village although, strictly speaking, the medieval religious foundation was a Priory, translated to this idyllic location from nearby Embsay in 1154.

Bolton Abbey

The Augustinian Canons, who owned the Priory with its enormous church and lands scattered throughout the Yorkshire Dales, derived most of their income from sheep farming and lead mining. By using lay brothers for these tasks, they were left with ample time to pursue their lives of prayer and study along with charitable works.

The Friars at Bolton were left undisturbed except for two occasions, the first in 1318 and the second two years later, when the Priory was attacked, ransacked and pillaged by that notorious Scottish Border Reiver, Black Douglas. Bolton Priory continued in existence until 1540 when it was closed by Henry VIII.

Although much of the valuable stone was plundered for new local buildings, the nave was left intact to serve as the parish church. In later centuries the Great Arch inspired several painters, notably Turner. Eventually the estate passed into the hands of the Dukes of Devonshire and, in more recent times, the present Duke has opened-up several miles of footpaths through the estate and by the River Wharfe. In addition he has signed access agreements with the Yorkshire Dales National Park covering many square miles of moorland.

Beamsley Hospital

Standing by the A59 trunk road and entered through an archway bearing a coat-of-arms, Beamsley Hospital was a refuge for homeless women rather than a place for the sick. It was established by Lady Margaret Clifford who was granted a charter by Queen Elizabeth I in 1593. The original part of the Hospital is based on a circular chapel with cottages fanning out from it and with a garden in between. It was restored in 1961 and is now owned by the Landmark Trust.

The Route

Leave the car park by the kiosk entrance and turn right along the road as directed by a footpath sign reading, "The Priory". At the Y-junction after only a few metres, veer left, so keeping the village green on your right. On reaching the B6160 cross directly to negotiate a small gate in what is known as "The Hole In The Wall".

Descend the following flight of steps before curving round to the left and heading towards the Priory ruins. Negotiate a kissing gate to use the well maintained path to Waterfall Bridge which spans the River Wharfe.

At the far end turn left but, after 20 metres, fork right up more steps

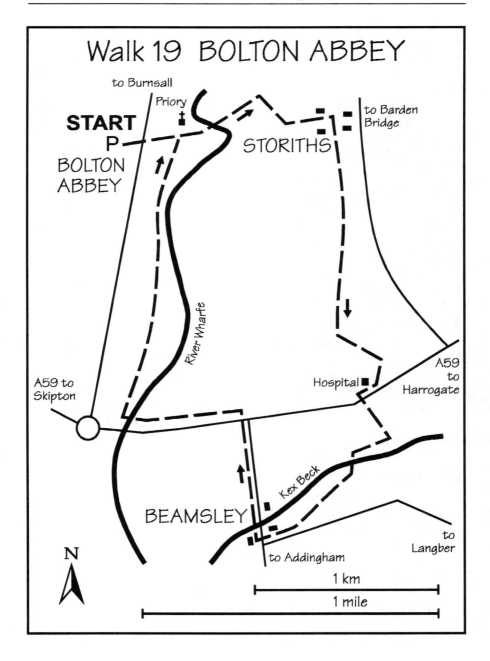

and continue upwards. A few metres beyond a wooden seat, and by a footpath post, make an acute turn to the right along a path signed to Storiths. Down below there is a delightful view of the Wharfe flowing through the verdant valley with the darker form of the Barden Moors forming the backdrop.

On reaching the top of the initial stretch of the climb there is a junction of paths accompanied by more footpath finger posts. Turn left through a small wooden gate onto a walled path flanked on both sides by green fields. In Summer this is lined by an abundance of foxgloves and other wild flowers. For a while the gradient eases before embarking on its final steep assault towards a gate which provides an exit onto a rough lane.

Make a left turn along this and stay with it as it works its way through Banks Farm and the tiny hamlet of Storiths to a T-junction. Cross directly to the facing stone step stile adjacent to a footpath sign and then bear right to a wooden five-barred gate. Through this turn sharply to the left to walk on the immediate right of a wall, passing under overhead wires to yet another footpath sign and a stone step stile.

Continue forwards through a 30-metres wide corridor formed by two stone walls and, at the far end, turn right and stay to the left of a wall. Where this curves away to the right, maintain your line of direction while aiming for a pylon carrying a faded yellow waymark. From this take a bearing on an obvious stone step-stile combined with a wicket gate in the facing stone wall and then continue forward to another stone step-stile immediately to the left of a small area of fencing.

Over this stile climb a small slope to a wooden gate located at the right-hand corner of an outbuilding of New Hall Farm. Advance to the left of the farmhouse before walking the partially surfaced track across a cattle-grid with a wicket gate adjacent. Stay with the track as it runs alongside Struff Wood and loses altitude before reaching the A59 by a footpath post.

Turn right along this busy main road for a very short distance to Beamsley Hospital. By this ancient monument turn left and cross the A59 to a footpath sign. Pass through the small gate alongside and remain to the left of a stone wall to negotiate two stone step-stiles before descending a very short slope to a T-junction by the bank of Kex Beck.

Turn right along the track, navigating a course between the stream on your left and a stone wall on your right. Continue beyond a corrugated metal barn on your right before the track narrows into a path and eventually reaches a concrete footbridge. Turn left across this and, at the far end, stay forward a short distance. Skirt to the right of several clumps of gorse for approximately 20 metres before turning right, up a slope, to a stile by a wooden pylon.

From there stay about ten metres to the left of another wall to a wooden stile and then turn right, advancing to the immediate left of another wall. The path now follows a course along the base of Beamsley Moor on your left until meeting a footpath sign and the minor road from the A59 to Beamsley Beacon.

Turn right for 100 metres to a T-junction. Go right again, passing through the hamlet of Beamsley with its moss-encrusted bridge over Kex Beck. Half a kilometre beyond the lane meets the A59. Turn left and, using the pavement on the northern side, head westwards for about 150 metres before turning right through a gap in the wall. On the far side turn sharp left along the narrow path which runs parallel to the road but which is separated from it by a wall.

Ignore the first footpath sign. Maintain direction over the old bridge and, at the far end, turn right through an iron kissing gate onto the wide riverside path which, with its grass surface, makes for some very pleasant walking.

Through a galvanised metal kissing gate the path acquires a fence on the right. Where the river bends, follow the path as it cuts a corner and proceed between a high bank on your left and the river on your right. Stay forward across the greensward aiming for the Priory which is now clearly visible ahead. On reaching that well-maintained path, turn left and retrace your steps to the Hole-In-The-Wall. The Tea Cottage is to the left by the Post Office.

Walk 20: Storiths

A gem of a high moorland walk with sharply contrasting views.

Route: Cavendish Pavilion – Bolton Park Farm – Hammerthorn Gate – Hazlewood Moor – Pickles Gill – Noska Head – Storiths – Cavendish Pavilion.

Start: The Cavendish Pavilion car park, Bolton Abbey. Map reference 077553.

Distance: 5½ miles (8.7km)

Map: "Lower Wharfedale and Washburn Valley", number 27 in the O.S. "Explorer" series *or* "The Yorkshire Dales: Southern Area" number 10 in the O.S. "Outdoor Leisure" series.

Public Transport: Dalesbus service 800: Leeds – Bradford – Ilkley – Hawes. Summer Saturdays, Sundays and Bank Holidays. Also Tuesdays in late July and August. Keighley and District Bus Co.
Dalesbus service 800: Harrogate – Hawes. Summer Sundays and Bank Holidays only. Harrogate and District Bus Co.
Dalesbus service 899: Skipton/Ilkley – Grassington – Buckden. Summer Sundays and Bank Holidays only. Pride of the Dales Bus Co.

By Car: The Cavendish Pavilion is signed from the B6160, Bolton Bridge to Aysgarth road, a short distance north of Bolton Abbey. There is a large car park. Fee payable but the ticket may also be used on the same day for other car parks on the Bolton Abbey Estate.

The Tea Shop

In these days of honey-pot tourism it is a delightful surprise to discover a tea shop in the tiny upland farming settlement of Storiths, situated high above the River Wharfe overlooking Bolton Abbey.

Buffers Coffee Shop was built in 1683 – as a shippon. It continued to perform this function at Back 'o' th' Hill Farm until as recently as the late 1980's when Keith Blackburn and his wife, Pam, found the introduction of milk quotas a threat to their traditional livelihood. To plug the financial gap and so allow them to maintain their herd of pedigree

Canadian Holsteins, they converted the former shippon into a Coffee Shop.

It bears all the hallmarks of the late seventeenth century with its thick stone walls, deep-set windows and enormous wooden beams which have obviously stood the test of time. A more modern aspect is the model railway gallery where patrons may wander to see the trains in action as they speed through the model countryside lovingly created by Keith. If they share his enthusiasm they can purchase a variety of models including Hornby Dublo and "00". The Blackburns also sell a wide range of books on both railways, walking and the countryside.

Walkers who venture away from the riverside paths of Lower Wharfedale have also come to appreciate Pam's farmhouse cooking, especially her Fruit Pies with sinful helpings of cream, her home-made Soup and her Scones which virtually suffocate under generous portions of jam and cream.

Another of her specialities is the Set Afternoon Tea consisting of assorted sandwiches, scones, cakes and a pot of tea. The display of cakes, all home-baked on the farm, changes daily but is more than likely to include Chocolate, Lemon, Walnut, Coffee, Flapjacks and Millionaire's Shortbread.

Plainer fare comes in the form of sandwiches, both plain and toasted, Toasted Teacakes, Omelettes, Beans on Toast, Wensleydale Cheese or Jacket Potatoes. There is a choice of both speciality teas and coffees, not to mention soft drinks and ice-creams. Opening times: Daily, all year, 10.30am to 5.00pm. Phone 01756 710253.

Cavendish Pavilion

There is also a chance to eat at the Cavendish Pavilion near the start and finish of this walk. With its light, airy atmosphere, quarry-tiled floors, cream walls and plant displays it sports a floral atmosphere appropriate to its title. It offers a wide range of food and drinks including speciality teas and coffees, sandwiches, soup, jacket potatoes, and Daily Specials. Cakes embrace Chocolate, Walnut and Millionaire's Shortbread. There is also a selection of speciality preserves for sale. Opening times: Easter to late October: daily, 9.30am to 6.00pm. Winter: Saturdays and Sunday only. 9.30am to 6.00pm or dusk. Phone 01756 710495.

The Route

From the car park turn right by the Cavendish Pavilion to cross the

The Cavendish Pavilion

"Wooden Bridge" spanning the River Wharfe and, 100 metres beyond, cross the minor road to enter the track signed to Bolton Park Farm. Climb steeply for a short distance through the woods. Keeping to the left of the farm buildings, bear right by a footpath sign to negotiate a wooden five-barred gate. With the rocky summit of South Nab above to the left, continue upwards on a wide chatter track as the gradient eases to a second wooden five-barred gate.

On the far side the track bears leftwards across the upland pastures where, in Spring and early Summer, the calls of the cuckoo, curlew and golden plover may be heard. In due course the wide track crosses two cattle grids to Hammerthorn Gate, a spot recognised by another wooden five-barred affair on the edge of the moorland.

Immediately through this there is a junction. The chatter track goes off to the left. Ignore this. Instead take the right-hand path, staying forward along a wide, partially grassed track, which courses through the heather over the summit of Hammerthorn Hill at 340 metres with moorland vistas on all sides.

After curving round to the right, the track arrives at a T-junction by a large, square boulder. Turn right to cross Hazlewood Moor and Cowmes Hill with nothing but moorlands in sight. The peat surface provides excellent walking before the track corkscrews down the slope to the head of Pickles Gill. After passing a stone sheepfold on your right and fording the beck, embark on another ascent with a fascinating view down the upper reaches of Pickles Gill on your right.

At the next T-junction, located just below Pike Stones to the left, turn right. Pass a short distance to the left of the very isolated Intake Farm to reach a footpath sign. Stay forward in the direction of Storiths. After a further 500 metres reach a Y-junction. Again turn right, still following the sign to Storiths.

The track begins to lose altitude gently as it runs along Gill Bank and by Noska Head to an inverted Y-junction with a footpath finger post.

Bear left, still in the direction of Storiths. From this point onwards the track provides a sharp dividing line between the moorlands on the left and the green fields on the right and there are occasional glimpses of Bolton Park Farm and the Cavendish Pavilion down below to your right.

Stay to the right of a five-barred wooden gate and continue a further 250 metres to another footpath sign. Maintain direction along the rough track, cross a cattle grid and continue through a gateway with a Barden Moor Access Panel nearby. A further 300 yards beyond this brings the track to a surfaced road. Turn right. Ignore a cul-de-sac on the left and continue through Storiths to Back O' Th' Hill Farm. Suitably refreshed stay with the road as it descends steeply towards the Wharfe. Having crossed the ford, or the adjacent wooden footbridge, bear left onto the riverside path which leads directly back to the Wooden Bridge. Turn left over this to regain the Cavendish Pavilion.

Walk 21: Barden Bridge

After partnering the River Wharfe, this route climbs green lanes to
cross Appletreewick Pastures with their debris of lead mining
before returning by way of Trollers Gill and Howgill Lane.

Route: Barden Bridge – Dales Way – Woodhouse Farm – Kail Lane – New
                     Road – Parcevall Hall – Higher Skyreholme – Howgill – Barden
                     Bridge.

Start: The parking area by Barden Bridge. Map reference 053574.

Distance: 10 miles (16.1km)

Map: "The Yorkshire Dales: Southern Area", number 10 in the O.S. "Out-
                     door Leisure" series.

Public Transport: Dalesbus service 800: Leeds – Bradford – Ilkley – Hawes. Summer
                     Saturdays, Sundays and Bank Holidays and Tuesdays in late July
                     and August. Keighley and District Bus Co.
                     Dalesbus service 899: Skipton – Grassington and Buckden. Summer
                     Sundays and Bank Holidays only. Pride of the Dales Bus Co.

By Car: Barden Bridge is on the minor road which leaves the B6160 at Barden
                     Tower for Appletreewick. The B6160 runs from Bolton Bridge on the
                     A59 to Threshfield. Parking is alongside the river at the eastern end
                     of Barden Bridge.

The Tea Shop

There is a genuinely medieval feel to the atmosphere in the tea rooms
at Barden Tower which is situated a few metres up the road from the
start and finish of the walk. Housed in the former Priest's House of this
historic complex, it has a rough wooden ceiling supported by gigantic
oak beams, thick stone walls with small, deeply inset windows, and two
extremely large fireplaces, one adorned with kettles and saucepans, and
the other housing a log-burning stove.

There is a grandfather clock and two Welsh Dressers with their racks
of patterned serving dishes, all sufficiently large to hold a side of beef.
The rough, wooden doors are fastened by snecks and the main decora-
tions are dried flowers and paintings of Barden Tower and Barden

Bridge. When the weather is fine refreshments are also served outside in the grounds.

There is a daily selection of lunches but Tower Broth, Cumberland Sausages with Mustard Dip, Hunting Lodge Pate, Scotch Woodcock or Braised Oxtail in red wine almost invariably figure. Sandwiches come in various sizes such as "Dainties", "Doubles" or "Wedges".

For mid-afternoons there is a choice between Lady Anne's Tea or Cream Tea, and the selection of home-made cakes includes, amongst many others, Scones, Marzipan and Apple Crumble, Baked Ginger Pot, Curd Tart and Cream, Coffee and Walnut Sponges.

All these may be washed down by a variety of teas such as Earl Grey, Sri Lankan Golden or Fruit. Similarly there is a range of coffees plus Horlicks, Hot Chocolate and Iced Coffee. Opening times: Easter to October: Wednesday to Sunday, 10.30am to 5.30pm. Also Tuesdays during July, August and September. Open during the Christmas and New Year season. Phone 01756 720616.

The Tea Rooms, Barden Tower

Barden Tower

Barden Tower, which is remarkably well preserved, was the most important of the six hunting lodges built in the Forest of Barden. It was enlarged in 1485 by the tenth Lord Clifford who was known as "The Shepherd Lord". Later, in 1658, it was restored by Lady Anne Clifford who was also responsible for similar work on a string of castles between Appleby and Skipton. It now belongs to the Devonshire Estate.

Parcevall Hall

According to local tradition this splendid Tudor building was once used by the nefarious highwayman, William Nevisson. On one occasion, having committed a crime at Gad's Hill in Surrey, he is alleged to have ridden to York in less than fifteen hours. To substantiate his alibi he immediately joined the Mayor of York in a game of bowls. His feat, which is said to have inspired the story of Dick Turpin's ride on Black Bess, so impressed King Charles II that the monarch described him as "Swift Nicks".

Today Parcevall Hall is a Retreat and Conference Centre for the Diocese of Bradford. Although the house is closed to the public its 16 acres of gardens and woodlands, including a wide variety of unusual plants and shrubs not normally seen growing so far north, are open to visitors. Opening times: Daily from Easter to October from 10.30am to 5.00pm. Phone: 01756 7203111.

The Route

From the end of the parking area furthest away from Barden Bridge, take the narrow path which runs in a northerly direction to the left of the wall and road and to the right of the River Wharfe. After 150 metres, and by a footpath post, join the main track which is signed to Howgill.

This riverside path is a section of the Dales Way, a long distance route which runs for more 80 miles from Ilkley to Windermere. Accompanied all the way with enticing views of the Barden Fells and passing through the delightful Haugh Wood, stay with the riverside path for approximately 4km to Woodhouse Farm.

A few metres beyond, turn right into the lane which leads, after a very short distance, to the Burnsall to Appletreewick road. Cross directly into Kail Lane, a sunken bridleway flanked by embankments which are topped with hawthorn bushes and signed to "New Road".

Initially it climbs steeply onto the northern shoulder of Kail Hill from where it offers a splendid view of Hartlington Hall on your left. As the gradient eases it develops into a walled lane, bends to the right and

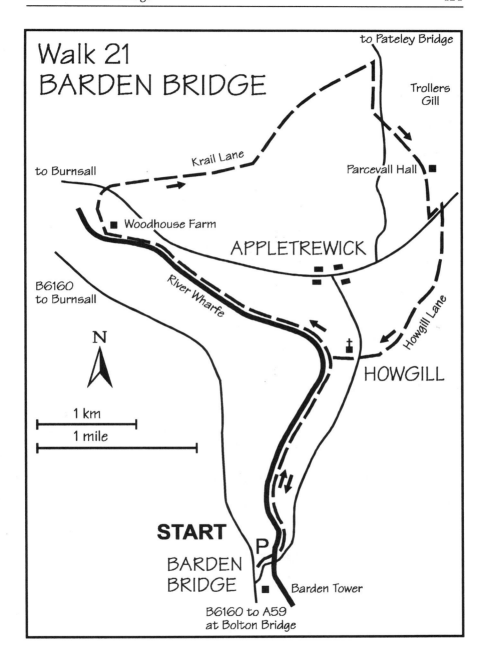

Walk 21
BARDEN BRIDGE

to Pateley Bridge

Trollers Gill

Krail Lane

to Burnsall

Parcevall Hall

Woodhouse Farm

APPLETREWICK

B6160
to Burnsall

River Wharfe

N

Howgill Lane

1 km

1 mile

HOWGILL

START
BARDEN
BRIDGE

P

Barden Tower

B6160 to A59
at Bolton Bridge

passes Dib Side. From this vantage point the rocky summit of Simon's Seat is easy to detect in the far distance ahead and there is another tantalising prospect down the clough through which the River Dibb flows on its way from Grimwith Reservoir.

By a stone barn at Kail Gate Laithe, the lane curves sharply to the left before crossing Appletreewick Pastures with their disused mine workings. For a short distance the wall on the right is lost but re-appears after the track passes through a five-barred gate.

At a cross-roads in the path network maintain direction along the wide lane for a further 100 metres to another gate. Through that, continue for a few metres to a finger post. Turn left along the signed bridleway with its firm, chatter surface. The bridleway soon reaches a ladder stile adjacent to a gate and then, quite surprisingly, passes to the left of a large, partially-buried fuel tank. It continues across a stretch of rough moorland dotted with more abandoned mine workings until it emerges onto New Road.

Turn right along this for 350 metres before going left over a ladder stile onto a path signed to Skyreholme. Aim for the ridge on the distinct path before descending gradually as you enjoy a fine view down into Trollers Gill on the left. Beyond a ladder stile the line of the path is marked out by two parallel rows of spasmodic hawthorns.

Pass above a field barn to a wall which clings to the contour. Turn right, negotiate a stile set into the facing wall in the field corner and then turn left again before losing more altitude to meet a broad path which accompanies Skyreholme Beck as it flows from Trollers Gill.

Turn right along this to pass through a gateway and stay forward to the driveway to Parcevall Hall. Turn left over the bridge. After 50 metres, and in front of two cottages, turn right over a somewhat obscure step stile set into the corner to follow a field path to the left of the wall.

Beyond a gateway head for a second and then turn right immediately through a third gateway. Drop down the field to reach a stile which permits access to a minor road at Skyreholme Bank. Turn left for the climb to Higher Skyreholme, a distance of approximately 400 metres. By a footpath finger post on the left, turn right through the opposite gate. Walk between the buildings to a second gate before crossing a field, taking your direction from the arm of the finger post adjacent. Cross Blands Beck by the footbridge in the field corner, aim for another step stile set into the wall on the right about half way along the field boundary and which is located at the spot where some pig wire, running along the top of the wall, comes to an end.

Maintain your direction through another gateway and to the left of a derelict barn to reach Howgill Lane. Turn right along this, soon passing Eastwood Head Farm with Simon's Seat now directly above to your left.

Continue along Howgill Lane for more than a kilometre. 100 metres beyond the entrance to Howgill Lodge Barn and Camp Site, and at an intersection in the path network, turn right down another lane. This loses height as it descends alongside How Beck for half a kilometre to reach the road at Howgill. There, cross to the footpath sign and turn left along the Dales Way path. With the Wharfe on your right, retrace your steps along the riverside path to Barden Bridge.

Walk 22: Burnsall

*Passing through the attractive heart of Wharfedale this route
reveals the different facets of the landscape of the Dales.*

Route: Burnsall – Badger Lane – Skulbert's Hill – Thorpe – Dowgill – Hebden
                     Suspension Bridge – Loup Scar – Burnsall.

Distance: 3¾ miles (6.2km)

Start: Car park, Burnsall. Map reference 032611.

Map: "The Yorkshire Dales: Southern Area", number 10 in the O.S. "Out-
                     door Leisure" series.

Public Transport: Dalesbus 800. Harrogate to Hawes. Summer Sundays and Bank
                     Holidays only. Harrogate and District Bus Co.
                     Dalesbus 800: Leeds – Bradford – Ilkley – Hawes. Summer Satur-
                     days, Sundays and Bank Holidays. Also Tuesdays in late July and
                     August. Keighley and District Bus Co.
                     Dalesbus 899. Skipton – Ilkley – Grassington – Buckden. Summer
                     Sundays and Bank Holidays only. Pride of the Dales Bus Co.

By Car: Burnsall is on the B6160 from Bolton Bridge to Threshfield. It is
                     signed from the A59 at Bolton Bridge. There is a Pay and Display
                     car park by the village green in Burnsall.

The Tea Shop

As the name implies, the Wharfe View Tea Rooms opposite the village
green in Burnsall, command a fine vista across the valley of the River
Wharfe to the Barden Fells beyond. The white stone walls, adorned with
paintings of local scenes which are for sale, provide a very relaxing
atmosphere. The wooden tables are surrounded by spindle-backed
chairs.

   The Afternoon Tea includes a choice of sandwich, a scone with jam
and cream and a home-made cake from the trolley, followed either by
a pot of tea or a cup of coffee. High Tea consists of gammon, two eggs,
chips, pineapple and bread and butter.

   For those suffering real hunger there is home-made Steak and Kidney

Pie, Soup with a Roll, or the All-Day Breakfast which is definitely one of the finest served anywhere in the Dales.

In addition Wharfe View also offers Original Welsh Rarebit, Yorkshire Rarebit with Ham, a choice of Omelettes or salads, Ploughman's Lunch or a selection of sandwiches. Drinks embrace a variety of speciality teas and coffees as well as hot chocolate and mineral waters. Opening times: Summer: daily 9.30am to 5.30pm. Closed Friday. Winter: 9.30am to 5.30am. Closed Thursday and Friday. Phone: 01756 720237.

Burnsall

Burnsall is a worthy mecca for all who wish to explore this section of Wharfedale on foot. The extensive village green, complete with maypole, nestles by the banks of the river with the Barden Fells providing a dramatic backcloth.

The main street, lined with seventeenth and eighteenth-century houses of mellowed stone with their mullioned windows, climbs to the parish church of St Wilfrid. Parts of this venerable building date from the twelfth century but its original foundation may have been much

Burnsall Bridge, over The Wharfe

earlier. In the churchyard there are some Viking Hog-Back tombstones and Norse crosses dating from the ninth and tenth centuries. Despite its early roots, the present church is, for the most part, constructed in the Perpendicular style of the sixteenth century.

Inside there is a memorial tablet to Sir William Craven, a native of nearby Appletreewick who, like Dick Whittington, found the streets of London paved with gold. Having amassed a fortune as a mercer and draper, he became Lord Mayor but never forgot his Yorkshire roots.

He paid for extensive repairs to St Wilfrid's, funded the building of the elegant arched stone bridge which still carries the road over the Wharfe at Burnsall and established the Grammar School which not only still stands, but serves as the village Primary School. One unusual feature of the village is the lych-gate leading to the church because it has a very rare turnstile entrance.

The village green is the traditional venue for the Burnsall Sports which have been held annually without interruption since the days of Queen Elizabeth I.

The Route

Leave the car park by the main entrance. Turn right along the B6160, soon passing the maypole on your right and the Wharfe View Tea Rooms on your left. On reaching the T-junction facing the "Red Lion" and by Barden Bridge, turn left following the road as it bends sharply to the right.

A few metres beyond this bend and by a footpath finger post indicating a route to Thorpe, turn left through a small wooden gate alongside a stone cottage. Advance 15 metres to a second gate before crossing a narrow field to a gated stone step stile.

Maintaining the same line of direction, cross the next field to a second gated stone step stile which permits access to a narrow lane. Cross directly to a wooden stile in the facing fence before continuing through five further narrow fields with stone step stiles before reaching a second track.

Pass through the gap in the facing fence and proceed across the field to yet another stone step stile by a wall corner. Beyond, advance some 10 metres to the left of a stone wall and then continue under some overhead wires and over a large, open field to the wall corner. Maintain the same line of progress for a further 25 metres to the immediate right of a wall before making a left turn over a gated stone step stile. Then climb slightly with another wall some 25 metres to your right.

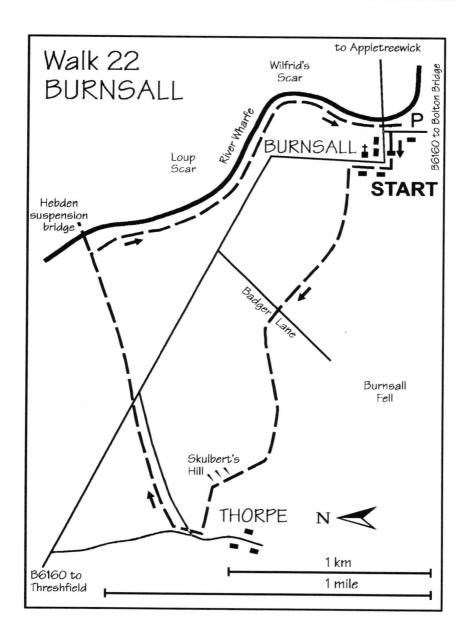

Walk 22
BURNSALL

to Appletreewick

Wilfrid's Scar

B6160 to Bolton Bridge

River Wharfe

Loup Scar

BURNSALL

P

START

Hebden suspension bridge

Badger Lane

Burnsall Fell

Skulbert's Hill

THORPE

N

1 km

1 mile

B6160 to Threshfield

From the crest of this rise bear left towards a wooden pylon and a footpath sign adjacent to a gated stile which grants entry to Badger Lane. Cross the lane to a gated stile and advance to the left of a wall until arriving at a two-armed finger post.

Veer left, as directed, but remain to the right of a row of trees. The clear, distinct path traverses a large field some distance to the left of yet another line of trees to a gated stile with a footpath sign adjacent.

Cross the next field to a gated stile before heading towards the southern end of the tree-covered Skulbert's Hill. Descend the grass slope to negotiate a wooden footbridge and then climb 5 metres to a gated stone step stile.

Proceed to the left of a stone wall as it curves to the right, around the base of Skulbert's Hill to a small wooden gate. Through this remain to the right of a stone wall along a broad, grass path as it climbs slightly by some limestone outcrops. At the summit turn acutely to the left to pass through a wooden five-barred gate into a walled lane. Proceed along this but, by a waymarker, corner right and, still with the lane, negotiate a five-barred gate to reach a T-junction with a footpath finger post. The tiny settlement of Thorpe is but a few metres to your left. Turn right along the partially surfaced lane, losing altitude as it twists and turn to pass Dowgill Laithe before meeting the B6160.

Cross directly to a small wooden gate by a bridleway sign and, after passing through, stay to the left of a wall to a wooden stile adjacent to a wooden five-barred gate. Maintain direction, still with a wall on your right for a short distance, as the broad, clear path crosses a large field. Beyond the next small gate a succession of waymarker posts reveal the line of the path as it descends steeply to another footpath sign alongside a small wooden gate. This provides access to the riverside path by Hebden Suspension Bridge.

Turn right, pass through another gate, cross a small wooden footbridge and climb a stile as the well-maintained path clings to the western bank of the River Wharfe. After a short distance the path climbs very slightly as the river flows through a mini limestone gorge formed first by Loup Scar and then by Wilfrid Scar. Continue alongside the river the reach Burnsall Bridge and, just beyond the village green, the car park.

Walk 23: Grassington

The outward route crosses rich limestone pastures before climbing through a woodland nature reserve to be followed a relaxing stroll along the banks of the River Wharfe.

Route: Grassington – Cove Lane – Grass Wood – Ghaistrill's Strid – Sedber Lane – Grassington.

Start: National Park car park, Grassington. Map reference 004637.

Distance: 5 miles (8km)

Map: "The Yorkshire Dales: Southern Area", number 10 in the O.S. "Outdoor Leisure" series.

Public Transport: Services 71, 72 and 272: Skipton to Grassington. Mondays to Saturdays. Pride of the Dales and Keighley and District Bus Companies.
Dalesbus 800: Leeds – Bradford – Hawes. Summer Saturdays, Sundays and Bank Holidays. Also Tuesdays in late July and August. Also from Harrogate on Summer Sundays. Keighley and District Bus Coy and Harrogate and District Bus Co.
Service 24: Harrogate – Pateley Bridge – Grassington. Summer Sundays and Bank Holidays. Harrogate and District Bus Co.

By car: Grassington is on the B6265 from Skipton to Hebden. It is also signed from the B6160 road at Threshfield. The Yorkshire Dales National Park has provided a large Pay and Display car park adjacent to the National Park Offices on Hebden Road.

The Tea Shop

The Dales Kitchen on Main Street, Grassington, is a genuine haven of Yorkshire hospitality housed in a stone cottage which, in turn, has served as an apothecary's shop, miner's cottage and stable block. Its two, small but welcoming rooms are furnished with pine dressers and a display of silk flowers. On sale is an intriguing array of tea pots, home-made preserves, teas and other gifts.

For the ravenous there is Black Sheep Rarebit, made with Masham's famous ale, sandwiches with various fillings including Roast Ham or

Oak-Smoked Salmon, home-made Lamb and Aubergine Moussaka and Spinach and Feta Filo. The soups, which change daily, include such unusual brews as Apple and Parsnip. Defiers of cholesterol will be delighted by the extra-large scones smothered in jam and cream or the Sticky Toffee Pudding or the Blueberry and Marzipan Pie or the delectable Chocolate Cake or the many other temptations which tend to change on a daily basis.

To round-off any meal, large or small, or no meal at all, there is a range of speciality teas, coffees and soft drinks. Opening times: Daily, including Sundays, all year. 10.00am to 5.00pm. Phone 01756 753208.

Grassington

With its country shops, cobbled Market Square, narrow streets and stone houses, Grassington has long been a major tourist mecca in the southern area of the Yorkshire Dales. An hour spent exploring the village on foot will repay handsome dividends.

Walkers are drawn to Grassington by the variety of routes radiating out from the centre. These range from all-day strenuous walks to short riverside rambles such as the one to Linton Falls on easy, well-trodden and well-waymarked paths.

The village lies at the junction of several ancient trackways across the Dales, many of which were of monastic origin. The village also benefited from the construction of turnpike roads during the eighteenth century.

By that date it had also evolved as an important centre for the lead mining industry, rich ore deposits being worked throughout the local countryside, especially on Grassington Moor which was owned by the Duke of Devonshire. The relics of this industrial activity may still be discovered by the observant walker. Its historical importance is perhaps best gauged by the fact that in 1282 it was granted the privilege of holding a weekly market. This survived until the nineteenth century when it finally ceased trading.

It is curious for a village of such importance that Grassington has never enjoyed the benefits of a parish church. Along with the neighbouring villages of Threshfield and Hebden it has always been served by St Michael's which is to be found about half a mile distant at Linton, close to the celebrated Falls.

Grassington is now one of the two centres for the administration of the Yorkshire Dales National Park, the other being at Bainbridge in Wensleydale.

Linton Church

Grass Wood

Grass Wood, along with the adjacent Bastow Wood, is an important nature reserve owned by the Yorkshire Wildlife Trust. It is all that remains of the vast forest which once covered much of Wharfedale. It is noted for its limestone flora and is rich in bird life. In the southern section a collection of mounds are the remains of a medieval village which became deserted after the Black Death killed most of its population. A public footpath runs through the reserve but visitors are requested not to pick the flowers and to respect the wildlife.

A plaque on the old Smithy in Main Street, Grassington, commemorates Tom Lee who was hanged for murdering the village doctor in Grass Wood.

The Route

From the car park entrance turn left into Hebden Road. After 200 metres turn right into the village centre, passing through the cobbled square and continuing up Main Street to pass the Post Office. By the Town Hall fork left into Chapel Lane towards Town Head, passing the Methodist Church on the way.

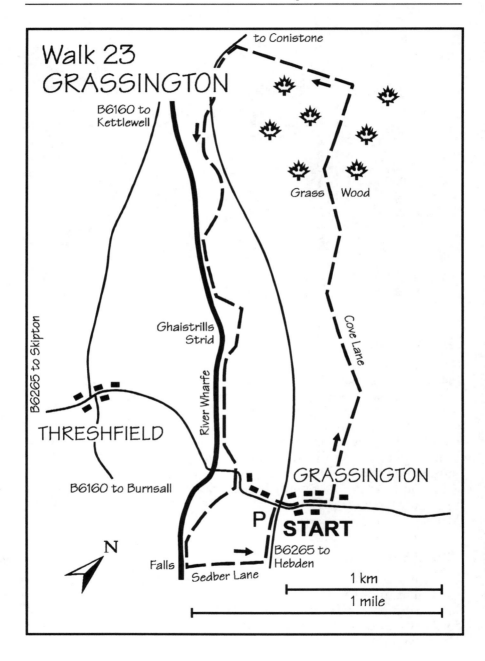

Walk 23
GRASSINGTON

to Conistone

B6160 to
Kettlewell

Grass Wood

B6265 to Skipton

Ghaistrills
Strid

River Wharfe

Cove Lane

THRESHFIELD

GRASSINGTON

B6160 to Burnsall

P START

N

B6265 to
Hebden

Falls

Sedber Lane

1 km

1 mile

Where the road bends acutely to the left, stay forward to a footpath finger post indicating a route to Conistone.

Enter the farm yard but, by the cattle pens, turn left to another finger post. Pass between more cattle pens to a small wooden gate adjacent to a metal five-barred one. Negotiate this and proceed for approximately 8 metres to another footpath sign, this time with 2 arms. Bear left towards an obvious squeezer stile and yet another footpath sign from where there is a good view up Wharfedale.

Stay forward, taking your direction from the arm of the footpath post to cross a triangular-shaped field, keeping to the right of a solitary tree with a crumbled stone structure at its base. Advance to the right of a series of small knolls to another footpath sign by a stile in a field corner. Turn left through this stile to join Cove Lane on a bend. Make a right turn along this walled lane to pass a series of field barns. Notice the distinctive limestone terracing on the right which rises up to Gregory Scar.

Where the lane terminates, by another footpath sign and a broken metal five-barred gate, maintain direction over a narrow field while staying to the immediate right of a wall to a gateless gateway with yet another footpath sign. From there bear diagonally right to a conspicuous ladder stile on the boundary of Grass Wood.

Climb this stile to be greeted in Spring by a chorus of woodland birdsong provided, amongst many others, by blackbirds, robins, thrushes, blue tits, great tits, tree creepers, chaffinch, fieldfares and redwings with a frequent solo by the drumming woodpecker.

Initially the path rises gently through the mixed deciduous woodland, which also boasts the occasional Scots Pine, to a somewhat inconspicuous Y-junction. Fork right, so staying with the broader path as it continues and steepens its climb for several hundred metres before levelling-out and meeting a four-armed finger post.

Ignoring the side paths, stay ahead along the path signed to Grass Wood Lane. It is much wider and loses altitude quickly before eventually reaching an unsigned T-junction. Turn left, proceeding down hill to a stile alongside a wooden five-barred gate and a footpath sign.

Negotiate the stile and turn left along the minor road for some 500 metres. Opposite an obvious ladder stile on the left, turn right through a kissing gate to follow the path signed to Grassington. Take the well maintained path which soon curves left to run alongside the River Wharfe. Pass through some trees while climbing about 75 metres above the river before losing height to return to the water's edge.

From this point onwards continue along the fine, springy turf with the Wharfe on your right, negotiating a stile and passing through a gateway before forking right for a view of Ghaistrill's Stryd where the water pulsates through a narrow rocky channel. Remain with the well-trodden path as it negotiates several stiles and wooden gates before finally leaving the river as it heads towards the left-hand end of Grassington Bridge and the B6265.

Exercising extreme caution, cross the road directly to a facing through stile with a wicket gate to join the riverside path signed to Hebden and Burnsall. Just beyond a planked footbridge over a side stream, there is an enormous weir to your right, soon to be followed by the Linton Falls.

Opposite these, negotiate a wooden footbridge with a stile at the far end to emerge onto Sedber Lane. Turn left for the climb up this flagged bridleway, passing through one of two kissing gates alongside each other, one of the old-fashioned metal variety and the other wooden. The choice is yours.

Where the gradient levels, and by a footpath sign, veer left into the car park from which you started.

Walk 24: Kilnsey

This high level route offers excellent walking and superb views of Central Wharfedale.

Route: Kilnsey Trout Farm – Conistone Bridge – Conistone – Wassa Hill – Scot Gate Lane – Old Pasture – Bastow Wood – Conistone – Conistone Bridge – Kilnsey Trout Farm.

Start: Kilnsey Park and Trout Farm. Map reference 974676

Alternative Start: Conistone village. Map reference 982675.

Distances: From Kilnsey Park: 7 miles (11.2km); From Conistone: 6¼ miles (10km)

Map: "The Yorkshire Dales: Southern Area", number 10 in the O.S. "Outdoor Leisure" series.

Public Transport: Dalesbus 800: Leeds – Bradford – Ilkley – Hawes. Summer Saturdays, Sundays and Bank Holidays and Tuesdays in late July and August. Keighley and District Bus Co.
Dalesbus 809: Keighley – Skipton – Leyburn. Fridays in late July and August. Keighley and District Bus Co.
Dalesbus 899: Skipton – Ilkley – Buckden. Summer Sundays and Bank Holidays. Pride of the Dales Bus Coy Service 71, 72 and 272 : Skipton – Grassington – Buckden. Mondays to Saturdays. There are no buses to Conistone. Alight at Kilnsey and walk to Conistone.

By Car: Kilnsey Park and Trout Farm is located on the B6160 north of Threshfield and south of Kettlewell. Parking at Kilnsey Park and Trout Farm is intended for visitors and patrons only.
Conistone village is signed from the B6160, a very short distance south of Kilnsey Crag. Alternatively it may be approached by a signed but unclassified road from Grassington. There is limited off-road parking opposite the Chapel and Hostel, a few metres south of the village centre.

The Tea Shop

Not surprisingly, there is considerable emphasis placed on trout, both fresh and smoked, at the tea shop in Kilnsey Park and Trout Farm.

However, this does not mean that it excludes all else. There is Battered Fish and Peas, Yorkshire Ham and Eggs, Soup of the Day, Rabbit Fricassee, Venison Casserole, Lasagne, Quiche Lorraine, Steak Pie and Bacon, Sausage and Egg. In addition there is a selection of sandwiches or filled baguettes, while for that afternoon treat the range of home-made cakes is absolutely bewildering and includes Fruit Crumble, Treacle Tart, Apple Pie and a whole range of cakes. The Cream Tea consists of a choice of Trout or Cucumber sandwiches followed by a scone smothered in cream and preserves.

The magnificent views of Kilnsey Crag and the central reaches of Wharfedale make this an ideal place to round-off a good walk, especially as there is outdoor seating for those fine, sunny days. The interior has a light, airy atmosphere with its tiled floors, beamed roof, white walls, wooden tables and spindle-backed chairs. Opening times: daily, all year: 9.00am to 5.30pm. Phone 01756 752150.

The Tea Room, Kilnsey

Kilnsey Park and Trout Farm

Kilnsey Park and Trout Farm owes its existence to a spring of pure water flowing from the overlooking hillside close to the celebrated Kilnsey

Crag. During the medieval period it was owned by the monks of Fountains Abbey who, like the present owners, used it to farm fish. More recently it was used to power an electric generator for the village until it was made redundant by the arrival of the National Grid. Since then it has been developed, mainly as a trout farm but with several other attractions added. These include fishing, fun fishing for children, an adventure playground, a conservation and nature trail and a Dales Life Centre with its aquarium of freshwater fish and other displays.

The Route

If starting from Kilnsey Park and Trout Farm walk south along the B6160 to the first road junction. Turn left to cross the road bridge spanning the Wharfe and continue into the centre of Conistone village. Join the route from Conistone by turning left towards the church.

Alternatively, if starting from Conistone, walk northwards for approximately 200 metres from the parking area opposite the Chapel and Hostel to the village centre. At the junction fork right to pass the parish church on your left.

Approximately 100 metres beyond the church fork right into Scot Gate Lane, a bridleway signed to Middlesmoor, some eleven miles distant in Nidderdale. With Kilnsey Crag clearly visible away to the left, this walled lane embarks on a long, steep climb. Pass through a small gate adjacent to one of the metal five-barred variety and continue ascending until level with a TV mast on Wassa Hill.

From this vantage point there is a vast panoramic view of the upland plateau with its many limestone outcrops. The air is filled with the calls of the curlew, lapwing and golden plover and the incessant song of the skylark.

After a short, level stretch, Scot Gate Lane resumes climbing to pass through another five-barred metal gate before reaching a four-armed footpath sign. By this turn right through a very small wooden five-barred gate onto a path which forms a section of the Dales Way. Within 15 metres, cross a stone footbridge with a steep-sided valley to your right. The wide, distinct path provides excellent walking as it traverses the green turf of this extensive upland plateau to a ladder stile with a three-armed footpath post. Stay forward in the direction of Grassington to another ladder stile. Maintain the same bearing to pass to the left of a lime-kiln which was restored in 1994 on your way to yet another ladder stile.

Beyond this bear slightly to the left, the most distinctive feature being

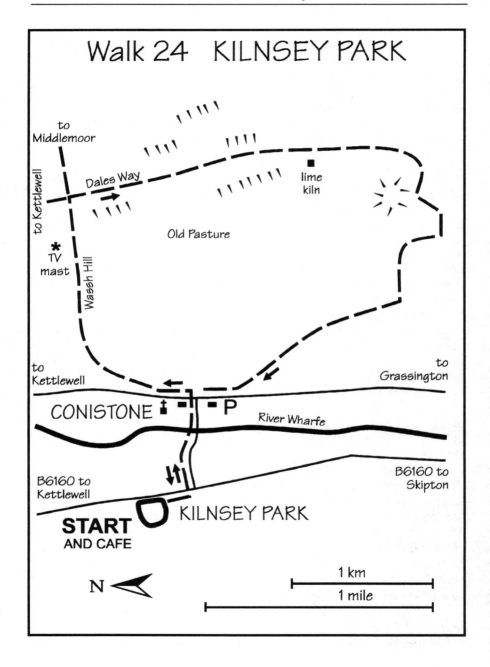

Walk 24   KILNSEY PARK

to
Middlemoor

to Kettlewell

Dales Way

lime
kiln

* TV
mast

Wassh Hill

Old Pasture

to
Kettlewell

CONISTONE

River Wharfe

to
Grassington

P

B6160 to
Kettlewell

B6160 to
Skipton

KILNSEY PARK

START
AND CAFE

N

1 km

1 mile

Sweet Side Ridge with its rocky outcrops, away to your left. Negotiate a small wooden gate before bearing slightly right through a derelict wall while aiming for an obvious ladder stile ahead. Immediately over this, leave the Dales Way by swinging right onto another wide but unsigned path which runs to the left of a limestone knoll towards a ladder stile in the facing wall. The boundary of Bastow Wood is a short distance to the left. Beyond the ladder stile turn right to a through stile in another facing wall after 100 metres.

Keeping an eye open for the early purple orchid, descend the very steep slope for approximately 60 metres to the head of Dib Clough and climb a similar distance to a stone step stile with a footpath sign adjacent.

Over this turn left and stay to the right of a wall. The path skirts the edge of Dib Clough, with patches of limestone pavement on your right. After losing a little altitude and traversing a short stretch of open slope with a steep drop to the left, veer right up the grassy hillside, guided by a series of waymarkers.

Eventually the going levels and the green swathe of a path clings to the right of a wall to reach a wooden five-barred gate in a wall corner. Stay forward to a hawthorn tree. By this veer slightly right to a footpath sign. Proceed along the same bearing while using another series of waymarkers to guide you across a very large pasture. From the next footpath sign go towards to a wooden five-barred gate, this time with a barn on the left.

Keep to the immediate right of another wall, losing height rapidly as the path develops into a wide track and passes through two more five-barred gates before meeting a walled lane. Turn left along this for some 20 metres to meet the road from Grassington to Conistone. Turn right for the short distance to the parking area opposite the Chapel and Hostel.

If returning to Kilnsey Park proceed a few yards further to the village centre where a left turn will carry you back to the B6160. Turn right for the short distance back to Kilnsey Park.

Walk 25: Kettlewell

An easy but rewarding exploration of Upper Wharfedale.

Route: Kettlewell – Paradise – Cross Wood – Starbottom – Haw Fields –
                      Kettlewell.

Start: Car park, Kettlewell. Map reference 968724.

Distance: 6 miles (9.5km)

Map: "The Yorkshire Dales: Northern and Central Areas", number 30 in
                      the O.S. "Outdoor Leisure" series.

Public Transport: Dalesbus 800. Leeds – Bradford – Ilkley – Kettlewell – Hawes.
                      Summer Saturdays, Sundays and Bank Holidays. Also Tuesdays in
                      late July and August. Keighley and District Bus Co.
                      Dalesbus 800. Harrogate – Leeds – Kettlewell – Hawes. Summer
                      Sundays and Bank Holidays only. Harrogate and District Bus Co.
                      Dalesbus 809. Keighley – Skipton – Kettlewell – Leyburn. Fridays in
                      late July and August only. Keighley and District Bus Co.
                      Services 71, 72 and 272. Skipton – Grassington – Kettlewell –
                      Buckden. Limited service on Wednesdays and Fridays only, all year.
                      Pride of the Dales and Keighley and District Bus Coys.
                      Dalesbus 899. Skipton – Ilkley – Grassington – Buckden. Summer
                      Sundays and Bank Holidays. Pride of the Dales Bus Co.

By Car: Kettlewell is located on the B6160 road which runs from the A59 at
                      Bolton Bridge to Aysgarth in Wensleydale. There is a large Pay and
                      Display car park by the bridge at the southern end of the village.

The Tea Shop

There is a genuine homely atmosphere about the Cottage Tea Room
opposite the car park in Kettlewell. The deep-set bow windows, with
their draped check curtains, frame spectacular views of Upper Wharfedale. The antiquity of the cottage is revealed in the beamed ceilings
with their rough wood and the stone fireplace, although a touch of
luxury is provided by the thick-piled carpets.

Jaynie and Michael Smith offer a menu that is without compare, not
only within the Dales but nationwide. Substantial items embrace
Ploughman's Lunch, Giant Yorkshire Puddings with Sausage or Beef

and Gravy, Egg and Chips and Home-made Soup The All-Day Breakfast is described as "The Best in the Dales". For lighter appetites there is a selection of salads and sandwiches.

Their Cream Tea consists of two scones with butter, cream and jam accompanied by a pot of tea. Jaynie and Michael's offering of home-made cakes makes the Devil's temptations look like the work of a novice. French Lemon Tart stands alongside mouth-watering Blueberry Pie while Apple Pie comes smothered in Cream. Toffee and Apple Cheese-cake vies with Hot Chocolate Fudge Cake while their Date and Walnut Loaf is a strong competitor with both Bakewell Tart and Carrot Cake.

The difficulties of choice do not end there because the large range of both speciality teas and coffees poses even more problems. Coffee is served in either cups or cafetières. Opening hours: April to October, daily: 9.00am to 5.00pm or even later if it is busy. November to March: Saturdays and Sundays only. 9.00am to 5.00pm. Phone 01756 760405.

Kettlewell

Ever since the medieval period when the three great abbeys of Foun-tains, Bolton and Coverham had estates in the area, Kettlewell has been a place of some significance in Upper Wharfedale. It enjoyed the

Top Mere Road, leading from Kettlewell to Cam Head

privilege of a weekly market and during the eighteenth and nineteenth centuries its wealth and prosperity were further enhanced by the development of the lead mining industry. In more recent times the village has become more or less completely dependent on tourism and agriculture. It is one of the most favoured walking centres in the Dales.

Starbottom

This tiny village has it roots in the Anglo-Saxon period and gains a mention in the Domesday Book of 1086. Later it became a centre for lead mining but a disastrous flood in 1686 completely demolished most of the houses. Few built before this date remain.

The Route

Exit the car park opposite the Cottage Tea Room and turn left along the B6120 to cross the hump-backed bridge. By the Bluebell Inn turn right and where the road bends round to the right, stay forward to pass between "Cam Lodge" and "Cam Cottage" into a lane. Within ten metres a sign indicates a route to Starbottom.

Climb gently for a short distance to a gated stile and then remain to the right of the stone wall which separates in-bye land from the upland pastures as it curves to the left. From this vantage point there is a fine prospect of Gate Cote Scar and up the valley of the Wharfe.

The line of the path is clear and easy to follow as it negotiates a succession of stiles, both ladder and traditional.

The slopes to the right are dotted with stunted, wind-blown hawthorns while the valley bottom, to the left, is littered with field barns. Pass Cross Wood, Paradise and several new plantations until, having negotiated a wooden gate, a two-armed footpath post is reached. Maintain the same line of direction along the contour to another, this time in a field corner.

Turn left through a gated stile before bearing right towards an obvious footpath sign half-way down the field by the right-hand wall. By this turn right through a gateway and proceed forwards for 20 metres to a second gateway before swinging left and then right to another footpath sign adjacent to a metal five-barred gate on the edge of Starbottom.

Pass to the left of "Foss Gill" and, after a further 10 metres and facing "Low Barn", turn left to meet the B6160 through Starbottom. Turn left along this. After 25 metres and by a footpath sign, turn right through a wooden five-barred gate into a walled lane which leads to a wooden

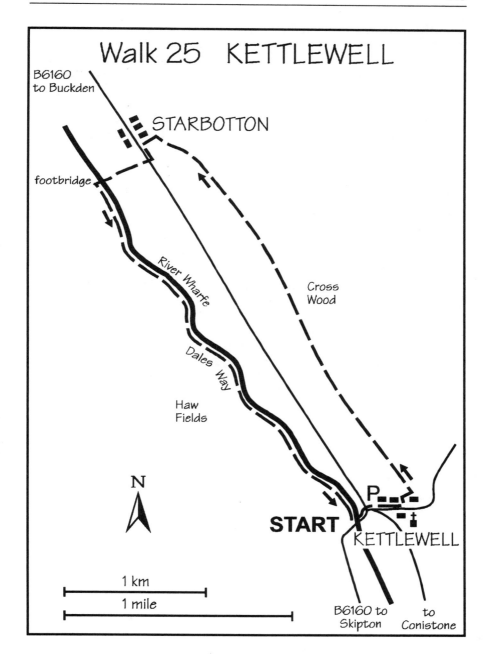

footbridge spanning the River Wharfe. At the far end, turn left through a squeezer stile to follow the riverside path signed to Kettlewell.

With the river on your left, aim for a stile by a gateway and then stay forward to another through stile. Ten metres beyond this climb a stile on the right but maintain direction to the right of a fence. After passing through a wall gap veer right to another stile with a gate alongside. In the next field swing further to the right, crossing a small footbridge over a stream, before bearing left to resume walking along the river bank.

Within a short distance negotiate another stile on the right but then turn left to stay alongside the Wharfe. Over the next stile veer right again to a five-barred gate before swinging left to another small footbridge.

From this aim for a stile some 20 metres to the right of a white gate and then stay forward to pick-up a wall on your right which forms the boundary of Haw Fields. Two ladder stiles in quick succession, followed by two wall gaps separated by only a few metres, lead to a five-barred gate from where the path develops into a broad, green track and, eventually, a walled lane.

After crossing a shallow ford turn sharply left through a wooden kissing gate onto a path that has a wall on the right and the river on the left. It is along this stretch of the Wharfe that sightings of both dipper and kingfisher may be enjoyed.

By a sign turn right through a gate, and then sharp left, to walk alongside a row of trees for 150 metres before turning left through another gate. Continue to the right of the river until the path passes a finger post to reach the B6160. Turn left for the final few metres to the car park in Kettlewell.

Walk 26: Buckden

A route for connoisseurs of fine walking and extensive panoramic upland views.

Route:　　Buckden – Cray – Scar House – Yockenthwaite – Hubberholme – Buckden.

Start:　　National Park car park, Buckden. Map reference 943773.

Distance:　　7½ miles (12km)

Map:　　"The Yorkshire Dales: Northern and Central Areas", number 30 in the O.S. "Outdoor Leisure" series.

Public Transport:　Dalesbus 800. Leeds – Bradford – Ilkley – Buckden – Hawes. Summer Saturdays, Sundays and Bank Holidays. Also Tuesdays in late July and August. Keighley and District Bus Co.
Dalesbus 800. Harrogate – Leeds – Buckden – Hawes. Summer Sundays and Bank Holidays only. Harrogate and District Bus Co.
Dalesbus 809. Keighley – Skipton – Buckden – Leyburn. Fridays in late July and August. Keighley and District Bus Co.
Services 71, 72 and 272. Skipton – Grassington – Buckden. Limited services on Wednesdays and Fridays only, all year. Pride of the Dales and Keighley and District Bus Coys.
Dalesbus 899. Skipton – Ilkley – Grassington – Buckden. Summer Sundays and Bank Holidays only. Pride of the Dales Bus Co.

By Car:　　Buckden is situated on the B6160 road some 19 miles north of Skipton. There is a large Pay and Display car park at the northern end of the village.

The Tea Shop

The splendours of the scenery in Upper Wharfedale are matched by the delights of the tea shop in Buckden which provides a fitting finale to the day's walk. West Winds Cafe, inconspicuously located behind the Buck Inn, is a true hidden gem. With its small-paned windows, thick stone walls, beamed ceiling, stone fireplace with its carved wooden top, floral curtains and carpets, it provides a snug and cosy atmosphere in the very heart of the Dales.

Proprietor Lynn Thornborrow ensures that all the baking is done by herself on the premises. The proof of the pudding, as they say, is in the eating and, put to this test, Lynn's cakes and pies will lead to a demand for a second helping. Her Fruit Pie, Treacle Tart, Chocolate Cake, Custard Tart, Coffee and Walnut Cake simply cannot be bettered.

Her scones, smothered in jam and cream, melt in the mouth. Her Afternoon Tea comprises sandwiches, scones with jam and cream, a selection from the cake display and a pot of freshly brewed tea. More substantial fare is offered in the form of Ham and Eggs, Meat Pie, Jacket Potatoes, Salads and Sandwiches. All these may be washed down·with a choice of teas, coffees, soft drinks or hot chocolate. Opening hours: Easter to October, daily 12 noon to 5.00 p.m. Closed Mondays. Winter. Open most week-ends, 12 noon to 5.00pm. Closed January and February. Phone 01756 760883.

Langstrothdale

North of Buckden Wharfedale changes its name to Langstrothdale, a famous medieval hunting ground. Today's landscape shows ample evidence of the enclosure movement of the late eighteenth century when the bare, open hillsides and lower pastures were divided into rectangular fields by hundreds of miles of drystone walls.

Originally, the area was settled by small Norse farming communities who have left their imprint in such names as Yockenthwaite. After the Norman Conquest much of the land passed into the ownership of Bolton and Fountains Abbeys as extensive sheep ranges. It was the monks who helped to create many of the green lanes which cross the district.

Hubberholme

Hubberholme is noted for the George Inn, converted from the former vicarage and a favourite of J.B. Priestly. A link with former times is maintained in the ancient ritual of "Letting the Poor Pasture", when local farmers bid for the tenancy of a field behind the pub on New Year's Day. The profits still help to maintain the poor of the parish.

The parish church of St Michael's and All the Angels, occupies an idyllic setting by the River Wharfe. It attracts visitors for all four corners of the globe. Originally a hunting chapel, it is thought to have been built on a former Anglo-Norse burial ground. The earliest reference to this church dates from 1214. Its Rood Loft is one of only two still surviving in Yorkshire, having been transferred from Coverham Priory in 1558, shortly after the Dissolution of the Monasteries.

The Route

Having negotiated the gate at the northern end of the car park, embark on the long gradual ascent of the bridleway signed to Buckden Pike and Cray High Bridge. One of the most historic routes in the Dales, it originated as a section of the Roman road linking the forts at Ilkley and Bainbridge. It climbs through the scattered remnants of a woodland, parts of the surface appearing to have been paved with sets at sometime in the past. For a considerable distance the bridleway is unfenced but 100 metres before the first five-barred gate acquires a wall on the left. Once through this gate the going eases and the countryside becomes far more open with superb views of Upper Wharfedale and Langstrothdale Chase which are ample reward for the strenuous initial climb.

By a second five-barred gate there is a junction. A path signed to Buckden Pike heads away to the right. Ignore this. Instead stay forward through the gate. The broad, well-defined path stays close to the wall on the left. The surface becomes transformed into an excellent springy turf which results in relaxed walking.

A third gate is instantly recognised by the massive limestone boulder that has been pressed into service as a gatepost. Beyond this, the wall on the left disappears, so maintain a line of direction to a stile from where the wall is picked-up once again.

75 metres after the stile turn left through a small gate onto a narrower but still distinct path which descends the slope to meet a wall on the right. Remain to the left of this but, by a wall corner with a footpath sign alongside, turn right. Continue losing height until fording Cray Beck opposite the White Lion at Cray. Cross the road and, following the track behind the pub and staying to the right of some farm buildings, pass through a five-barred gate to enter a farmyard. Continue through a second facing gate, ignoring one on your right. After a further 7 metres ford a shallow stream and pass more farm buildings to a three-armed footpath post. Do not go to the left. Instead advance for a further 25 metres to a gate and a sign indicating a footpath to Scar House and Yockenthwaite. Follow a distinct path high above Wharfedale to provide some breathtaking views of the heart of the Yorkshire Dales.

Beyond a waymarked gateway aim for a waymarked wall corner before proceeding to a waymarked wooden five-barred gate close to a field barn. Pass to the left of this barn before rounding a waymarked wall corner to another footpath post. Setting your direction by the arm of this, stay to the left of a wall which runs along the top of a small embankment on your right. On your left is Todd's Wood.

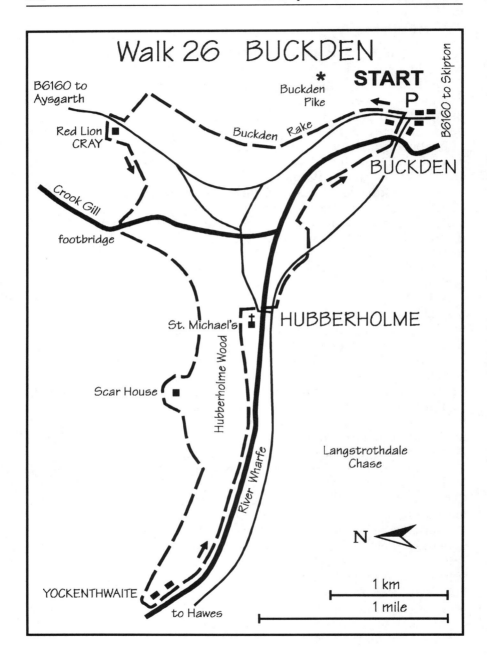

After approximately 150 metres perform a U-turn over the sturdy wooden footbridge spanning Crook Gill before advancing to the right of a low stone wall on an excellent turf path. This section of the route is designed by nature for sauntering while admiring the breathtaking views of Langstrothdale which rival those of Paradise. Buckden Pike is one of the obvious landmarks while Hubberholme Wood is closer to hand on your left.

The path runs along an upland grassy belvedere graced by several areas of limestone pavement and rocky outcrops while, a considerable distance down below, the infant Wharfe courses its way through the folds of moorlands like a silver ribbon glistening in the sun.

After a considerable distance the path curves in a semi-circle behind Scar House before descending several limestone platforms to a three-armed footpath post. Detour to the left of Scar House for a view of the front with its plaque over the doorway which reads:

"T

I.A.

1696

REBUILT 1876"

This isolated yet substantial residence, originally constructed for a

Scar House, Hubberholme

Quaker family, is now owned by the National Trust which is currently debating its future use.

Return to the footpath post and turn left to continue in your original direction which is now signed to Yockenthwaite. The path continues curving leftwards to a stone step stile adjacent to a five-barred gate. Over this it remains to the left of some trees while crossing exposed areas of limestone pavement and offering more high quality upland walking partnered by further magnificent views of this most central areas of the Yorkshire Dales. Kirk Gill Moor and Horse Head Moor dominate the skyline to the left.

Pass through a gated stile to enter a corner of Rakes Wood, now owned by the National Trust and consisting mainly of deciduous trees with a scattering of Scots Pines. Exit the wood by a footbridge with a stile at both ends and turn left to a stone step stile. Cross more limestone scars and outcrops to another stile quickly followed by a third. Beyond this the route is waymarked. After passing to the left of a stone barn, perched a little way above on the hillside, keep a sharp eye open for a yellow arrow painted low down on a derelict wall. By this turn left, losing altitude as the path descends the slope.

On reaching a facing wall turn right, as signed, staying with the contour across the hillside until reaching a track. Turn left for the final steep descent into the tiny hamlet of Yockenthwaite.

At the T-junction by Top Farm turn left onto the Dales Way. Proceed in front of the farm house, and pass through a gateway before advancing a further 20 metres to a gated stile. Through that turn right to a through stile and then sharp left onto the riverside path which has the Wharfe on the right.

Stay alongside the river, passing through a series of stiles until, a short distance beyond a barn, the paths appears to be blocked by a wire fence. There turn left through a small metal gate and then, after a further ten metres, make a right turn through a gateway and head for the waymarked gap.

At the far end of a wooden footbridge aim for a waymarked stile some 25 metres to the left of a five-barred gate and stay alongside the Wharfe until the square, squat tower of Hubberholme church comes into view.

Pass to the left of the church to a signpost. Turn right to a gate and then cross the old stone bridge over the river until meeting the lane alongside "The George". Turn left into the lane which, initially, partners the Wharfe.

By Grange Farm, which is on the right, the river bends away to the left. Continue along the lane until, 200 metres beyond a barn, a sign indicates a route to Buckden Bridge. Turn left through the five-barred gate onto a surfaced track and remain to the right of the wall until reaching the river. Here, make right turn as the path loses its surface and develops into a well-trodden green swathe along the right-hand bank of the Wharfe until it meets a minor road by Buckden Bridge. Turn left for the final 150 metres to "The Buck" and, just behind, "West Winds", where those well-earned refreshments will be waiting.

Walk 27: Malham

A visit to several of Malham's geological features.

Route: Malham – Janet's Foss – Gordale Bridge – Malham Cove – Malham.

Start: The National Park car park, Malham. Map reference 891627.

Distance: 5 miles (8km)

Map: "The Yorkshire Dales: Southern Area", number 10 in the O.S. "Outdoor Leisure" series.

Public Transport: Daleslink 580. Ingleton – Settle – Malham. Summer Saturdays and Bank Holidays only. Bibby's Bus Co. Links with the Settle-Carlisle trains at Settle.
Dalesbus 804/5. Leeds – Bradford – Malham – Settle – Hawes. Summer Sundays only. Keighley and District Bus Co.
Postbus: Skipton – Malham. Mondays to Fridays all year.

By Car: Malham may be reached by a minor road signed from the A65 in the centre of Gargrave. There is a large Pay and Display car park by the National Park Information Centre on the southern edge of the village.

The Tea Shop

The Malham Cafe occupies a commanding position in the centre of Malham village overlooking the beck. The present building, a former farm, dates from 1690 although it is believed that an earlier structure stood on the site. Its age is betrayed by its thick stone walls and massive oak beams. The floor is quarry tiled while the tables, chairs and benches are all constructed of wood.

With its no-frills menu it is obviously accustomed to catering for walkers in search of serious nourishment. Amongst many items on offer are the All Day Breakfast, Sausage, Egg, and Beans on Toast, Cornish Pasty, Cheese and Onion Pasty and Steak and Kidney Pie. As usual there is a choice of sandwiches, either hot, cold or toasted. For "Afters" there is a range of cakes on display in the cabinet and these include such favourites as Chocolate, Coffee and Lemon. Apart from coffee and tea both Bovril and Hot Chocolate feature on the beverages list. Opening

Cottages, Malham

times: 9.00am to 5.00pm, daily all year. Closed Mondays and occasionally Thursdays. Phone 01729 830348.

Malham

Long before the National Park was even a concept Malham was a tourist mecca, visitors attracted by its geological wonders including Janet's Foss, Gordale Scar, Malham Cove, the limestone pavements and Malham Tarn. Janet's Foss is named after the queen of the local fairies and the pool at the foot of this pretty waterfall was used by generations of farmers as a sheepwash.

Gordale Scar resulted from the collapse of a gigantic cave system and the two-tiered waterfall at its head is a major spectacle after heavy rainfall. Malham Tarn is one of only two natural lakes in the limestone areas of the Yorkshire Dales, the other being Semerwater in Wensleydale. It was formed by a natural rock hollow beneath which is a bed of impervious Silurian slate.

One of the main attractions is Malham Cove, an enormous natural amphitheatre which forms part of the Craven Fault. It is topped by an extensive limestone pavement consisting of flat blocks known as

"Clints" and intersected by deep fissures or "Grikes". The grikes, formed by persistent water action, are famous for their wild flora.

The Route

Exit the car park by turning left into the village. Opposite the "Buck Inn", cross the stone footbridge spanning Malham Beck before making a right turn onto the footpath signed to Janet's Foss and Gordale Scar. This runs through a succession of water meadows that are a botanist's paradise in Summer.

After two stiles and immediately through a kissing gate a junction is reached. Make a left turn onto the path signed to Janet's Foss.

This skirts to the left of a stone barn before continuing with a wall on the right to another kissing gate. Beyond this the sequence of stiles leads to the entrance of Janet's Foss Woodlands. Since 1982 these have formed part of the National Trust's Malham Tarn Estate. They consist mainly of ash and hazel which have regenerated naturally since the last Ice Age.

In Spring they are carpeted with wild garlic and dog's mercury, otherwise known by a variety of names including "Sweethearts", "Adam and Eve" or "Cuckoo Pint". They flower in April or May, subsequently developing clusters of poisonous red berries.

Continue along the well maintained path through the woodlands as far as Janet's Foss. Climb the path to the left of the waterfall before emerging onto Gordale Lane. Turn right along the road to Gordale Bridge. 300 metres beyond, and by a sign, turn left onto another surfaced path leading into the very heart of Gordale Scar, one of the most impressive sites in the whole of the Yorkshire Dales.

Having walked as far as the foot of the waterfall, retrace your steps to Gordale Lane. Turn right and proceed to Gordale Bridge. There leave the road by turning right through a wooden kissing gate onto a path signed to Malham Cove.

Aim for the first wall corner, a distance of some 50 metres, afterwards remaining close to the wall on your right for the stiffish climb up the pasture. Beyond a tall ladder stile bear right to a flight of steps leading to a footpath post with another kissing gate alongside. New Close Knotts are on your right.

Through the kissing gate turn left and stay to the right of a wall as the gradient eases. The path leads to a small wooden gate after which bear left while remaining to the right of the wall. After a further ascent the path again levels to pass a barn on the left by Cawden Fields. A short

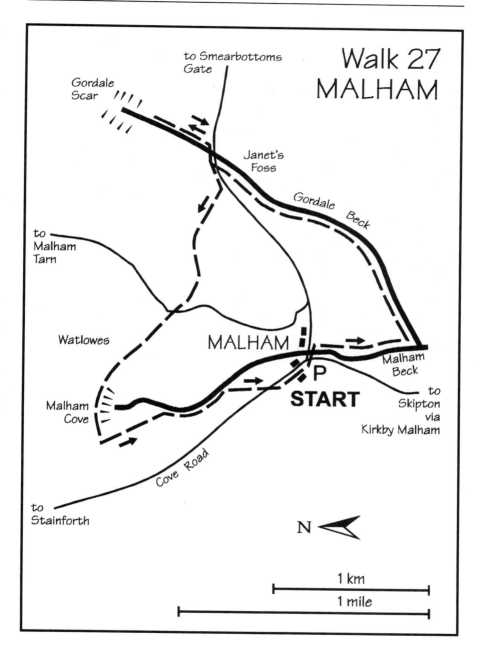

Walk 27
MALHAM

to Smearbottoms Gate

Gordale Scar

Janet's Foss

Gordale Beck

to Malham Tarn

Watlowes

MALHAM

Malham Beck

Malham Cove

P
START

to Skipton via Kirkby Malham

Cove Road

to Stainforth

N

1 km

1 mile

distance beyond resume your upwards course for a superb view down Airedale, with Lancashire's Pendle Hill visible in the far distance.

Eventually the path ceases climbing but twists and turns across the high ground on its way to a gate which permits access to the road at Malham Raikes. Turn right but, because of the acute bend, exercise extreme caution.

After approximately 5 metres make a left turn over a ladder stile onto a clear but stony path signed to Malham Cove, half a mile away. Initially there is another slight climb onto a green plateau dotted with numerous limestone scars and small patches of pavement to create a beautiful landscape. Once it has crested the summit, the path develops a grass surface which provides much needed relief to the feet and makes for extremely pleasant walking.

Eventually the path meets a wall on the left. By the corner of this bear gradually leftwards to a ladder stile alongside a gateway with a footpath sign adjacent. To your right is the attractive Watlowes Valley. From the stile continue forwards across the extensive limestone pavement above Malham Cove. At the far end turn left over either of the two ladder stiles for the descent of the long flight of steps. On reaching the floor of the Cove fork right at the next junction and follow the surfaced path. After several gates this reaches Cove Road where a left turn down the hill leads directly into Malham village, with its café and car park.

Walk 28: Settle

A strenuous but exhilarating exploration of the limestone
landscape around this famous Yorkshire town.

Route: Settle–Mitchell Lane–Lambert Lane–Sugar Loaf Hill–Warrendale
                       Knotts – Attermire Scar – Victoria Cave – Clay Pits Plantation –
                       Settle.

Start: Ashfield car park (Pay and Display), Settle. Map reference 819637.

Distance: 5$\frac{1}{2}$ miles (8.75km)

Maps: "The Yorkshire Dales: Southern Area", number 10 in the O.S. "Out-
                       door Leisure" series *or* "The Forest of Bowland and Ribblesdale",
                       number 41 in the O.S. "Outdoor Leisure" series.

Public Transport: Frequent trains from Leeds, Skipton and Carlisle. Daily, all year,
                       including Sundays.
                       Bus service 580. Skipton – Settle. Several daily except Sundays.
                       Pennine Bus Co.
                       Bus service 581. Ingleton – Settle. Daily except Sundays. Bibby's
                       Bus Co. Daleslink 580. Ingleton – Settle – Malham. Summer Satur-
                       days and Bank Holidays only. Bibby's Bus Co.
                       Bus services 110/111. Clitheroe–Slaidburn–Settle. Tuesdays only,
                       all year. Hyndburn Transport.
                       Dalesbus 804/5. Leeds – Bradford – Skipton – Settle – Hawes.
                       Summer Sundays and Bank Holidays. Keighley and District Bus Co.
                       Bus service X8. Ambleside – Kendal – Kirkby Lonsdale – Settle –
                       Skipton – York. Wednesdays, Fridays and Saturdays all year. Cum-
                       berland Bus Co.
                       Bus service X9. Ambleside – Kendal – Kirkby Lonsdale – Settle –
                       Skipton – Bradford – Leeds. Tuesdays and Thursdays only, all year.
                       Cumberland Bus Co.
                       Bus service 200. Leeds – Bradford – Skipton – Settle – Lancaster –
                       Morecambe. Summer Saturdays and Bank Holidays only. Keighley
                       and District Bus Co.

By Car: Settle is now by-passed by the A65, Kendal to Skipton road, from
                       which it is signed between Ingleton and Long Preston. There are two
                       Pay and Display car parks close to the town centre.

The Tea Shop

Formerly an inn, Ye Olde Naked Man Cafe derives its name from the relief figure of a naked man hiding his credentials behind a date plaque as a protest about the ridiculous clothing fashions of his period. The first indication of the delights awaiting the hungry walker are signalled by the aroma of the freshly-baked bread issuing from the bakery on the premises. The bow windows, with their draped curtains, are indicative of the age of the building, and are matched by wooden tables and spindle-backed chairs.

This is not a place for people in a hurry because time is definitely required to study the wide choice of home-made cakes and gateaux on offer which includes Caramel Shortbread, Fudge Cake, Rich Chocolate Slice, Japonais, Oatmeal Crunch, Fruit Crunch, Currant Slice, Eccles Cake, Honey and Oat Slice, a variety of Meringues, Vanilla Slices, Fudge Cake and, of course, Scones smothered in jam and cream. There is an equally impressive list of coffees such as Cappuccino, Espresso, Kenyan, Columbian, Italian and French. These are matched by a choice of speciality teas.

In addition to Soup of the Day there is a selection of sandwiches, both hot and cold, with fillings which include Cumberland Sausage, Gammon and Bacon. Opening times: All year: daily (including Sundays), 9.00am to 5.00pm. (Wednesdays only 9.00am to 4.00pm.) Phone: 01729 823230.

Settle

Although Settle remained somewhat isolated until the construction of the Keighley to Kendal Turnpike in the eighteenth century, it has always been a focal point for the Upper Ribble Valley and the western areas of the Yorkshire Dales. Its busy, bustling market, still held every Tuesday, was first established by charter in 1249. The wooded slopes of Castleberg, site of a motte and bailey castle, provides a dramatic backcloth to the Market Square which is surrounded by many seventeenth and eighteenth-century buildings, their antiquity authenticated by the initials and dates above their lintels. Many are separated by narrow yards and courts.

There are several notable buildings including the impressive nineteenth century Town Hall, the Folly which dates from 1675 and boasts some fine Jacobean windows, and the Shambles with its two levels, one of shops and the other of houses.

Today the town is closely associated with the Settle to Carlisle Railway line which crosses some of the wildest and most spectacular scenery in England. Plans to close it several years ago were thwarted by the opposition from several conservation and amenity groups including the Yorkshire Dales National Park. Leaflets giving details of the history and architecture of Settle may be obtained from the Tourist Information centre which is housed in the former Town Hall. Phone: 01729 825192.

Railway Station, Settle

The Route

Leave Ashfield car park by the toilet entrance. Opposite is Spread Eagle House, the birthplace of Thomas Procter, a local painter and sculptor who lived there between 1753 and 1794. Turn right into Kirkgate, the ancient route used by the people of Settle to attend their parish church in neighbouring Giggleswick.

Continue to the junction with Duke Street, the main road through the town. Cross into Cheapside and pass to the right of the Tourist Information Centre to the Y-junction by the Trustee Savings Bank, site of the birthplace of the Reverend Ben Waugh, founder of the NSPCC.

By the bank, fork right into High Street, keeping the Post Office and

Library on your right. Cross Chapel Street before bearing left into Victoria Street, signed to Malham and Airton. Almost immediately the Folly is on your left. For a short distance the surface is cobbled.

By "Chandler's Cottage" bear left, still towards Malham and Airton, into Albert Hill, climbing steeply whilst passing old houses and cottages. By "Chapel House" fork right into Mitchell Lane which is signed as a cul-de-sac, thereby leaving the road to Malham. By this stage there is a fine view over the town of Settle with the dome of Giggleswick School providing a rather more distant landmark.

For a distance the going levels as the lane passes Settle High Water Treatment Works but soon the gradient increases sharply. Ignore a footpath sign on the right, continuing along the walled lane with Ingleborough coming into view to the north. After a long, steep climb, the gradient levels before a Y-Junction is reached.

At this point leave Mitchell Lane by forking left into Lambert Lane which is signed as a bridleway to High Hill Lane. The route now crosses the vast limestone plateau with Black's Plantation on the right.

After 200 metres bear left, there being no access along the gated track to the right. Lambert Lane undulates for almost one kilometre until, having passed the partially derelict Preston's Barn on the left, it reaches the Settle to Malham road, High Hill Lane, by a footpath sign.

Turn right but, after 100 metres and by the sign "Stockdale", fork left into Stockdale Lane, a bridleway signed to Malham. After the first 100 metres bend left, with the bridleway, but, after a further 100 metres, where Stockdale Lane itself bends acutely to the right, negotiate a facing ladder stile onto a footpath signed to Attermire Scar.

Once over the stile, walk to the left of a wall as the grass path climbs to the crest for a breathtaking view of Warrendale Knotts and Attermire Scar directly ahead. At 370 metres, the aptly named Sugar Loaf Hill, stands in the more immediate foreground. This is certainly the most dramatic approach to these famous landmarks. On a clear day, a glance over the shoulder will reveal the whale-back shape of Pendle Hill in the Lancashire stretch of the River Ribble.

Maintain direction along the distinctive grassy swathe of a path as it rounds the foot of Sugar Loaf Hill before bearing right to a footpath post. From here continue forward towards a wall, which comes in from the right, and then pass through a partially derelict gateway. Immediately turn ninety degrees to the left, heading for a stone step stile adjacent to a conspicuous three-armed footpath post. Attermire Cave is high above.

By the footpath sign turn right in the direction of Malham. After 200 metres, and just in front of a wall gap, turn left for a short, sharp climb of 200 metres alongside a wall before turning right over a ladder stile.

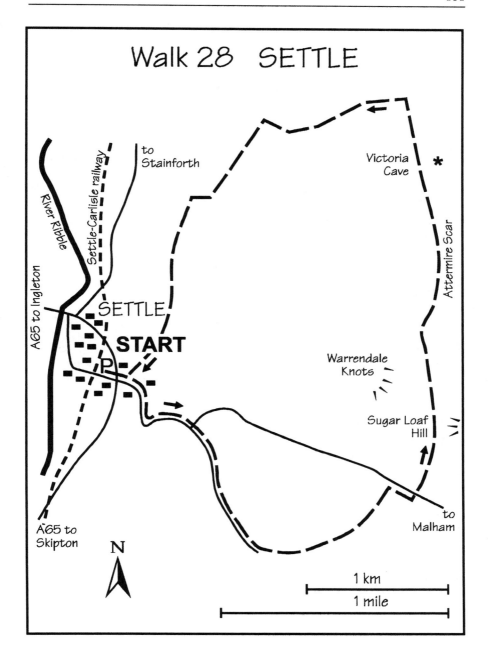

Walk 28 SETTLE

Turn left immediately, so maintaining direction but now on the right of the wall. In Spring and early Summer the call of the curlew fills the air while rooks fly overhead. Underfoot snails, their shells patterned with cream and brown swirls, cling to the rocks.

The path, initially very stony, levels after a further 150 metres to follow a course along the foot of Attermire Scar and acquires a grass surface as it traverses more open ground towards a wall corner on the right. Having rounded this, stay to the right of the wall with both Ingleborough and Robin Procter's Scar, near Austwick, conspicuous in the far distance. Brent Scar towers above on the right. Having negotiated a ladder stile, continue along the same bearing with a wall still on the left as you approach Victoria Cave. **Heed the warning notices**. Do not attempt to explore this or any of the other caves along the route. **They are dangerous**. Stay on the path.

After another ladder stile turn left to meet a rough track by a footpath sign. Again turn left, this time through a metal five-barred gate. Remain along this track as it descends to the right of Clay Pits Plantation with a good view of Stainforth Scar a short distance to the right.

100 metres beyond a cattle grid the track forms a junction with a minor road. By this junction turn left through a wooden five-barred gate onto a bridleway signed to Settle. Remain to the right of the boundary wall of Clay Pits Plantation but, by the far corner, bear slightly right towards a small wooden gate set between two enormous stone slabs.

Continue to the right of a wall to a second small wooden gate. Through this the path curves right to cross open pasture, initially staying with the contour before descending slightly to the right and meeting a third wooden gate.

On the far side of this, maintain direction along a good, grass path, now to the left of a wall, to a ladder stile on the right. Ignore this.

Instead continue forward, still with the wall on your right, until another wall draws closer from the left to form a corridor leading to a wooden five-barred gate. Having negotiated this, walk to the left of a wall to another wooden five-barred gate, adjacent to a derelict stone barn, which permits access to a walled lane. Continue along this until, having entered Settle, it develops into Constitution Hill.

At the end turn left into Bowskill's Yard to emerge by the Trustee Savings Bank. Turn right along your outward route to Duke Street and the Market Square where the aroma of freshly baked bread from Ye Olde Naked Man Cafe will be waiting to greet you.

Walk 29: Clapham

A route initially through parkland and then along field paths and green lanes with considerable geological interest and fine views.

Route: Clapham – Low Pond – Austwick – Town Head – Nappa Scar – Thwaite Lane – Summit Clump – Clapham.

Start: National Park car park, Clapham. Map reference 745693.

Distance: 4½ miles (7.3km).

Map: "The Yorkshire Dales: Western Area", number 2 in the Ordnance Survey's "Outdoor Leisure" series.

Public Transport: Clapham is served by daily trains from Leeds and Lancaster including Sundays. **Note:** Clapham station is approximately 1½ miles from the village.
Bus service 581. Settle – Clapham – Ingleton. Daily except Sunday, all year. Bibby's Bus Co. This connects with buses to Lancaster at Ingleton and buses for Skipton at Settle.

By Car: Clapham is by-passed by the A65 Skipton to Kendal road from which it is signed north of Settle. There is a large Pay and Display car park by the National Park Information Centre.

The Tea Shop

There is a real old-fashioned homely feel to the Brook House Cafe on Station Road in Clapham and a specially warm welcome for walkers. The café itself is housed in a typical cottage parlour which still retains its sash windows and fireplace. The green walls are decorated mainly with photographs.

Sarah Harrison caters for walkers with an enormous All-Day Breakfast embracing bacon, egg, sausage, hash brown, fried bread, tomato and beans. For those who cannot face such a gargantuan repast there is the Smaller Breakfast. Other dishes include egg on toast, egg and chips, cheese on toast and several vegetarian items. There is a choice of sandwiches, plain or toasted.

Omelettes, Chicken, Steak and Kidney Pie, Cumberland Sausage and Lasagne are also featured. Sarah's home-made cakes include Hot Chocolate Fudge, Lemon, Coffee and her Apple Pie is beyond compare. There is the usual range of beverages with a choice of speciality teas. Opening times: Daily, all year, 9.00am to 5.00pm. Closed Mondays except Bank Holidays. Phone 015242 51580.

Clapham

With old stone houses lining either side of the Beck, Clapham forms one of the most picturesque villages in the Yorkshire Dales National Park. It owes its eminence to its position on the Kendal to Skipton Turnpike and, in more recent times, as a starting point for the ascent of Ingleborough or for visits to the Ingleborough Show Cave or Gaping Gill pothole.

Originally an Anglian settlement, it is believed to date from the ninth century. 400 years later the Manor was granted to William de Clapham and in the nineteenth century this passed to the Farrer family. They remained as Lords of the Manor until shortly after the end of the Second World War.

Successive generations extended their landowning interests until their estate, comprising farmland, forest and moorland, became the largest in the North of England. Their ancestral home was Ingleborough Hall, built in 1840 and now serving as a outdoor educational establishment. The grounds were extensively landscaped, two tunnels being created so that the privacy of the family was protected from travellers along Thwaite Lane.

Reginald Farrer was a noted explorer and traveller who spent long periods in the Far East. He returned with many exotic Himalayan species which he planted on the estate at the head of a large artificial lake. Today there is a special Nature Trail open to visitors.(A Trail leaflet is available at the National Park Information Centre).

Austwick

The Scandinavian influence found throughout the Dales is evidenced in the name "Austwick" which is derived from the Norse word meaning "Easterly Settlement". The village itself is linear, consisting of attractive stone houses and cottages representative of every period from 1700. In the mid-sixteenth-century Austwick Hall was a fortified manor house, very much in the form of a Pele Tower designed to resist the marauding Scots and occupied by the Ingleby Family. The parish church has a most unusual dedication – "The Church of the Epiphany".

Robin Proctor's Scar

Robin Proctor Scar and Nappa Scar, both featured in this walk, consist of limestone formed beneath the sea millions of years ago from the shells of crustaceans and then raised to the surface as the climate changed. They are typical of several similar features found throughout the Dales and passed on several of these walks.

Robin Proctor Scar derives its name from a local farmer who, after an evening of revelry in the local hostelry, was riding along the top of the Scar when he met with a predictable accident. Another, apocryphal legend, tells how the folk of Austwick, fearful of it falling onto their village, tried to restrain it with iron chains.

Robin Proctor's Scar and Norber

The Route

From the Information centre, which stands close by the car park entrance, take the path signed to Austwick. This passes to the left of the toilet block and continues along the side of the car park to a small wicket gate. Alternatively join this path by negotiating the stile in the far right-hand corner of the car park and turning left.

Through the wicket gate continue in the same line of direction, with some farm buildings on your right followed by a fence, to a metal kissing gate adjacent to one of the five-barred variety. Maintain direction to the left of a metal fence to traverse the parkland of Ingleborough Hall with some well wooded slopes away to your left.

Beyond a second kissing gate the distinctive path clings closely to a fence on your right as it crosses a pasture to a third kissing gate in the facing wall. From there stay to the right of some trees to negotiate a fourth kissing gate before crossing the middle of an undulating field to a gated stone step stile.

Continue forward close to the wall on your right as the ground on your left slopes away upwards. Negotiate a second gated stone step stile adjacent to a wooden five-barred gate and maintain the same general line of direction after the wall corners away to the right.

Head across the open pasture to an obvious ladder stile which, unusually, has a stone step stile alongside, and then proceed to another pair of the same varieties before passing between a wall on your left and a clump of trees, complete with a rookery, on your right.

Within a few metres start to lose height to a stone step stile bearing a yellow waymark and cross the middle of the ensuing field where the path runs by a solitary tree with a seat alongside.

This particular field is of particular interest for landscape historians for the obvious terracing is, in reality, the lynchets or terraces once ploughed by our medieval forbears for the cultivation of arable crops. Even the changed patterns of agriculture and the construction of drystone walls during the early years of the nineteenth century, have failed to obliterate this evidence of a long-since abandoned agrarian system.

From this same field, too, are some extensive views over the lime-stone landscape which separates this area of the Dales from the region around Horton-in-Ribblesdale.

Over the next stile swing left and continue down the slope to pass between a bungalow and a house to a stile which facilitates access to the main road through Austwick.

Turn left and, opposite the church and by the telephone kiosk, fork left into the road signed to Horton. Pass the "Game Cock", the village school and a succession of attractive stone houses and cottages. By a house called "Hobbs Gate", turn left into Townhead Lane for a steepening ascent. Just beyond the last houses, and where the road bends sharply to the right, look for a ladder stile and adjacent stone step stile on your left. Over these, stay to the right of a wall while continuing to

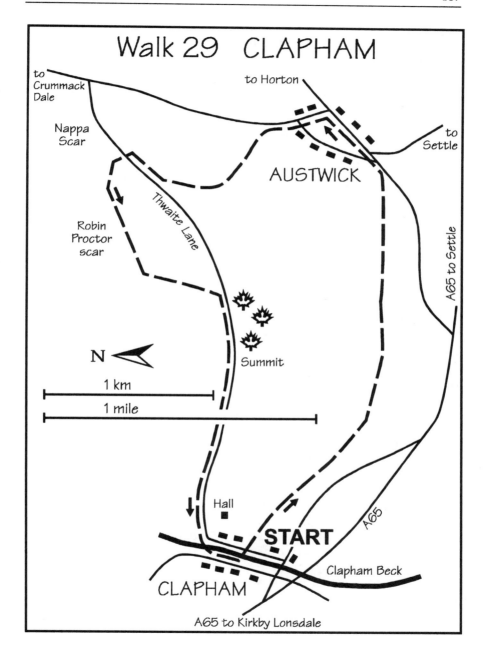

Walk 29 CLAPHAM

to Crummack Dale

to Horton

to Settle

Nappa Scar

AUSTWICK

A65 to Settle

Thwaite Lane

Robin Proctor scar

N

1 km

1 mile

Summit

Hall

START

A65

Clapham Beck

CLAPHAM

A65 to Kirkby Lonsdale

climb. In the Autumn there is always a scattering of fungi of various hues ranging from chestnut to white and including burgundy, yellow, green and lemon.

Follow the wall round as the gradient eases to a stone step stile in the field corner. Stay forward, initially to the right of the wall, and then across open land to a ladder stile which provides access to Thwaite Lane.

Turn right along this green lane for approximately 250 metres before climbing a ladder stile on your left to follow a wide, grassy track as it heads towards a wooden five-barred gate some distance ahead. Just before reaching this, however, the path swings slightly to the right to cling closely to a drystone wall which is on your left.

Negotiate a stone step stile adjacent to a locked wicket gate in the wall corner before continuing to climb towards the foot of Nappa Scar. Remain with this wall as it begins to curve left to reach a T-junction. Turn left, so staying close to the wall on your left with the impressive, jagged rocky face of Robin Proctor's Scar towering above on your immediate right.

After some considerable distance, negotiate a ladder stile and continue alongside the wall but, by a corner after some 50 metres, turn left across a large open field where the distinct, grassy path provides an excellent walking surface.

Pass to the right of a small area of limestone pavement before reaching a footpath sign and ladder stile to re-join Thwaite Lane. Turn right for an almost imperceptible climb along this walled lane, for centuries a well patronised packhorse route linking Lancaster with Richmond. It offers excellent panoramic views ranging from the distant rolling moorlands of the Forest of Bowland to Crummack Dale and Clapdale, with Ingleborough's flat summit close to hand.

After more than a kilometre pass Summit Clump, a small group of trees, before reaching a T-junction with Long Lane and its collection of finger posts. Continue forward in the direction signed to Clapham and, after a further 200 metres, embark on the steep descent and pass through two dark tunnels before emerging by Clapham parish church.

By the large gateposts of Ingleborough Hall, turn right into Church Avenue. Stay forward over the stone bridge spanning Clapham Beck to meet the main road. Turn left, walk to the right of the Beck for a short distance and then re-cross it by the old packhorse bridge to reach the car park.

Walk 30: Ingleton

A delightful route which, after an initial steep climb, crosses the limestone landscape before returning by the waterfalls.

Route: Ingleton – Fell Lane – Skirwith – Beezleys – Snow Falls – Ingleton.

Start: The main car park, Ingleton. Map reference 695730.

Distance: 4½ miles (7.25km)

Map: "The Yorkshire Dales: Western Area", number 2 in the O.S. "Outdoor Leisure" series.

Public Transport: Daleslink 580. Ingleton – Settle (connects with trains). Summer Saturdays and Bank Holidays only. Bibby's Bus Co.
Service 581. Settle – Ingleton. Mondays to Saturdays all year. Bibby's Bus Co.
Service 81. Lancaster – Ingleton. Daily except Sundays all year. Stagecoach Ribble Bus Co.
Service X8. Ambleside – Kendal – Kirkby Lonsdale – Ingleton – Skipton – Harrogate – York. Wednesday, Friday and Saturday, all year. Cumberland Bus Co.
Service X9. Ambleside – Kendal – Kirkby Lonsdale – Ingleton – Skipton – Bradford – Leeds. Tuesdays and Thursdays all year. Cumberland Bus Co.
Service 200. Leeds – Bradford – Skipton – Lancaster. Summer Saturdays only. Keighley and District Bus Co.

By Car: Ingleton is signed from the A65 Kendal to Skipton road which by-passes the village. There is a large Pay and Display car park adjacent to the Tourist Information Centre.

The Tea Shop

The cosy tea room is situated at the rear of the Curlew Crafts Gallery. Its exposed stonework walls are almost obliterated with a display of etchings, water colours and photographs mainly by local artists. There is soothing background music, floral tablecloths and fresh flowers on each table. Customers may even entertain themselves with tiny games of Solitaire.

Curlew Crafts Tea Shop

Chris and Sandra Bonsall provide an interesting and varied list of Daily Specials which may include Cheese and Onion Pie, Vegetable Soups of unusual combinations or leeks wrapped around with bacon in a cheese and mushroom sauce. At the end of a walk a Cream Tea is a must with Scones smothered in more than generous portions of jam and cream. The range of home-baked gateaux is almost too numerous to list but includes Banana Cake, Chocolate Cake, Walnut cake and Lemon Meringue Pie.

For an establishment with such an adventurous menu it is hardly surprising to discover an apparently endless selection of speciality teas and coffees. If the weather is favourable it is possible to eat and drink in the flower-filled courtyard. Opening times: July to October. Daily 9.00am to 6.00pm (5.30pm in September and October). October to June. Daily 9.00am to 5.00pm. but closed Wednesdays. Closed in January and the first two weeks in November. Phone 015242 41608.

Ingleton

Today it is almost impossible to believe but Ingleton once had a colliery employing in excess of 300 miners, working in difficult circumstances as they extracted coal from thin seams. The mine closed early in the twentieth century after a bitter dispute. The enormous viaduct spanning the valley is a reminder that Ingleton was formerly linked to both Settle and Sedbergh by a railway. Ingleton is recognised as one of the main starting points for an ascent of Ingleborough and is also a popular caving centre.

The Route

Leave the car park by the eastern exit and turn left along the road in the direction signed to Hawes. At the first road junction after 250 metres, turn right, still following the B6255 towards Hawes. Pass the Police Station and, where the road forks, go left, still with the B6255, now signed to Chapel-le-Dale.

After approximately 150 metres, by "Richmond House" and a footpath sign to Ingleborough, bear right up the bridleway, Fell Lane, which, initially, climbs fairly steeply. Eventually the gradient eases and the track develops into a walled lane.

Shortly after the going levels and by a footpath post, turn left over a tall ladder stile onto a field path signed to Skirwith.

Remain to the right of the wall to another stile, this time in the field corner as the path traverses open limestone country with White Scars close by on your right. Over this stile go left and then right to stay to the left of a wall while losing height to another ladder stile which provides access to the B6255.

Cross the road directly into what appears to be a lane but, after 5 metres, turn right through a small wooden gate and then left along a track. After 10 metres turn right over a small stone footbridge onto a path which runs parallel to the road.

Within 100 metres cross a second stone footbridge and turn right along the wide track around Skirwith Quarry. Remain to the left of a wall to a small wooden gate adjacent to a five-barred one.

Through that, turn left and follow the quarry road towards the traffic sign showing a white arrow on a blue background. By this, directed by a yellow waymark on a fence, bear right onto a track and, after a short distance, negotiate a ladder stile.

Over that head diagonally down a large, sloping field, gradually moving further away from the wall and plantation on your left.

The grass path eventually passes through a derelict wall and bends left to run downhill alongside a wall on your right, developing into a track as it does so. By a yellow waymarker post swing left to a wooden

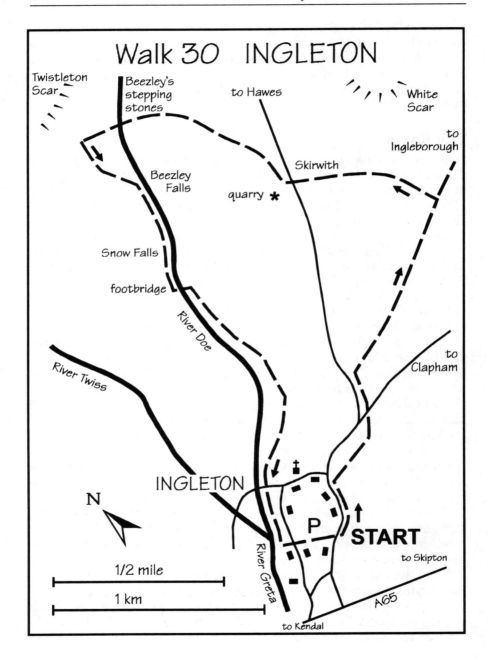

Walk 30   INGLETON

Twistleton Scar

Beezley's stepping stones

to Hawes

White Scar

to Ingleborough

Beezley Falls

Skirwith

quarry ✱

Snow Falls

footbridge

River Doe

River Twiss

to Clapham

N

INGLETON

to Skipton

P

START

River Greta

1/2 mile

1 km

A65

to Kendal

stile and, over this, cross the River Doe by the substantial stepping stones.

Continue along the track to Beezley's Farm. At the T-junction turn left, so keeping the white farm house on your right. Some 30 metres beyond, at a Y-junction and Beezley Falls sign, fork left onto a narrow path which, as it enters the woodland, becomes stepped.

It quickly leads down into a narrow, dramatic ravine where the River Doe tumbles over the Beezley Falls. Remain with this maintained path, which is a section of the famous Ingleton Waterfalls Walk. Heading downstream it passes the pretty Snow Falls and the North Craven Fault. Lower down it crosses the river by means of a footbridge before gradually climbing away to run to the right of a plantation and then into more open country. On the outskirts of Ingleton it becomes Thacking Lane. At the first junction fork left to reach High Street opposite the Post Office. Turn right along High Street which, in turn, becomes Main Street, for the final stretch to the Curlew Crafts and the nearby car park.